Research in Early Childhood

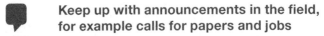

Research in Early Childhood

Andrea **Nolan**, Kym **Macfarlane** and Jennifer **Cartmel**

Los Angeles | London | New Delhi
Singapore | Washington DC

SAGE

Los Angeles | London | New Delhi
Singapore | Washington DC

SAGE Publications Ltd
1 Oliver's Yard
55 City Road
London EC1Y 1SP

SAGE Publications Inc.
2455 Teller Road
Thousand Oaks, California 91320

SAGE Publications India Pvt Ltd
B 1/I 1 Mohan Cooperative Industrial Area
Mathura Road
New Delhi 110 044

SAGE Publications Asia-Pacific Pte Ltd
3 Church Street
#10-04 Samsung Hub
Singapore 049483

Editor: Katie Metzler
Production editor: Sarah Cooke
Marketing manager: Catherine Slinn
Cover design: Jennifer Crisp
Typeset by: C&M Digitals (P) Ltd, Chennai, India
Printed and bound by MPG Printgroup, UK

© Andrea Nolan, Kym Macfarlane and Jennifer Cartmel 2013

First published 2013

Library of Congress Control Number: 2012951182

British Library Cataloguing in Publication data

A catalogue record for this book is available from the British Library

ISBN 978-0-85702-253-0
ISBN 978-0-85702-254-7 (pbk)

CONTENTS

LIST OF FIGURES

ABOUT THE AUTHORS

Associate Professor Andrea Nolan is a lecturer and researcher in the School of Education, Victoria University, Australia. Andrea has worked on a number of state, national and international projects concerning literacy development, program evaluation, and professional learning for teachers. Her research interests include the use of reflective practice as a way to enhance teachers' professional growth, early literacy, and early childhood pedagogy. She actively mentors higher degree students and early career academics undertaking research projects both within her university and beyond.

Dr Kym Macfarlane works at Griffith University, Australia, and has experience as an early childhood teacher and in higher education in the field of Child and Family Studies. Her research and publication work covers a range of topics related to the disciplines of human services and education. Kym's doctoral research encompassed philosophical and sociological perspectives on education and related to parent engagement in schooling. This work complements her early childhood knowledge and enables her to deliver teaching and research that is underpinned by multiple knowledge bases.

Dr Jennifer Cartmel, Griffith University, Australia, has a track record in research and practice with children and families, particularly in early childhood education and care and outside school hours care. She has used innovative and effective research methodologies with marginalised families and the associated family support workforce. Jennifer has extensive knowledge of the national quality reform agenda and the early childhood reforms, and networks with practitioners, researchers and policy makers in Australia and internationally.

RESEARCHERS FEATURED IN THIS BOOK

We have tried to give this book a different feel from other research books… it really tries to be like a mentor and friend. We want it to give you a sense of being with a group of people, sitting together talking about being researchers, and helping each other to understand what you need to know in plain English, or as plain as can be, about research terms and processes. To further enhance this feeling we have listed all of the researchers whose experiences we draw upon so that you can follow their journeys throughout the book. We begin by locating Lara and Amy, our featured doctoral students, and then list the other researchers in order of appearance.

Researcher	Experience	Chapter
Lara	Lara introduces herself and explains her initial interest in her topic. Also included in this chapter is her doctoral Abstract.	1
	Lara shares her thoughts on beginning her research.	2
	Lara highlights the complexity of the journey and suggests that research is an ongoing rather than a limited journey.	3
	Lara outlines her initial thoughts about topic areas and how her research project needed to be carefully considered so that it met the criteria and expectations of her scholarship.	4
	Lara discusses how she tackled her literature review and explains the evolution it went through.	5
	Lara comments about her use of phenomenology as a methodology and provides some hints about the process of preparing for, collecting and analysing data. She also highlights how she was very conscious about building a process to ensure her study's findings were reliable and valid. She offers advice for novice researchers.	7
	Lara describes the writing up of her thesis and her publishing aspirations.	9
	Lara reflects on her development as a researcher.	10
Amy	Amy is introduced and outlines what influenced her topic of choice. Also included in this chapter is her doctoral Abstract.	1
	Amy outlines her orientation to her research project. She provides a glimpse into her thinking about quantitative and qualitative methodologies and their strengths and differences.	2
	Amy discusses her interest in her topic which came from her personal experience of being a mother.	4

Researcher	Experience	Chapter
	Amy discusses how she grappled with whether to be selective or comprehensive in her coverage of the literature.	5
	Amy reflects on her own development during the research process, positioning herself as quite courageous in undertaking the thesis journey. She also looks to the future and research opportunities.	10
Maria	Maria, a doctoral student using narrative methodology, shares her experience of attending Master classes related to her methodology. We also read about her research and how she felt about engaging in research with children – rethinking methodology and methods to include the voices of children.	2
Rhys	Rhys, who is undertaking an introductory course in research methods, devised a way to try to understand the terms used in his research methods classes.	2
Sonia	Sonia, who is conducting research with school-age care services for a local government authority, tells her story of how she came to terms with applying a theoretical perspective to her study.	2
Sarah	Sarah, a doctoral student, illustrates some of the complexities involved in applying particular theoretical perspectives and aligning methodologies to answer certain research questions.	3
Janine	Janine, a researcher taking a qualitative approach to her research, discusses framing research questions.	4
Elizabeth	Elizabeth, a doctoral student in the early stages of her research journey, shares excerpts from her research proposal.	4
	In this chapter we hear about how she began writing her introduction, literature review and methodology sections of her thesis early on in the research process.	9
	Elizabeth's journey continues in this chapter, illustrating the importance of networking.	10
Sophie	Sophie, a social worker undertaking a Masters program, discloses the sensitivities regarding ethics and access that surrounded her study.	4
Karina	Karina, a mid-career researcher, outlines how she formulated questions that helped her to clarify and thereby shape her literature review.	5
Christine	Christine, an early career researcher, details how she managed materials for a literature review and also how she determined the point at which to conclude her literature search.	5
	Here, Christine writes about the dilemma which confronted her as she began interpreting interview data taking a qualitative approach.	7
	In this chapter we hear Christine's experience of developing a journal article from her doctoral studies findings.	9
Garrath	Garrath, a novice researcher, points to the dilemma of not organising information diligently.	5

(Continued)

(Continued)

Researcher	Experience	Chapter
Kiara	Kiara, a student undertaking a Masters degree, discusses how she positioned herself as a researcher and made a conscious decision to locate her own voice within her study.	6
Amber	Amber, an undergraduate student, relates her decision to use phenomenology as the research methodology and the multiple methods considered to incorporate the voices of the children in the study.	6
	In this chapter Amber talks about how she involved the children in authenticating her interpretation of the data by having respectful dialogue with the children about the mind maps she collaboratively created with them.	7
Andrea	Andrea, a mid-career researcher, recounts her experience of trying to ensure her data was valid and accurate for her doctoral study.	7
	In this chapter Andrea outlines the format she used to write up her doctoral thesis.	9
	Andrea explains how she was fortunate to link with an effective mentor early in her research career and how she now mentors other researchers.	10
Anne	Anne, in discussing her doctoral studies, provides an example of ethnocinema. Anne's research was represented by seven documentary films which comprised comment on the complexities of the identities for both researcher and co-participants.	9
Kristy	Kristy, a mid-career researcher, discusses how she went about disseminating information from a large government-funded study to a local audience.	9
Ali	Ali, an early career researcher, recounts his experience of being part of a large evaluation study where educationalists and healthcare professionals came together to ensure children's holistic development (education, health, welfare) was taken into account in the project.	10
Safira	Safira, an experienced researcher, talks about gaining a sense of who you are as a researcher within a research community.	10
Paula	Paula, an early career researcher, shares her thoughts on how she positions herself as a researcher and what has led to this positioning.	10
Jaymera	Jaymera, an early career researcher, positions herself as a critical ethnographer, providing her reasoning for this decision.	10
Kathryn	Kathryn, an early career researcher, discusses what has influenced who she is as a researcher.	10
Mira	Mira, who is studying an honours degree, outlines her decision to undertake an action research project and the direct impact that had on her practice.	10
Kym	Kym, an early career researcher, shares the steps she took to take her research journey forward after completing her doctoral studies.	10
Jennifer	Jennifer, an early career researcher, details how presenting at an international conference can be the start of ongoing networking opportunities.	10

ACKNOWLEDGEMENTS

This book would not have eventuated without the support of a number of people. We would therefore like to thank:

Anna Kilderry who helped conceptualise the initial concept of the book and her interest in its progress; Elizabeth Rouse who gave us permission to showcase her excellent research proposal; Annemarie Hindle for commenting on an early draft of the quantitative chapter, and Anthony Watt for his reflections on a later version of the same chapter; our families for their understanding, allowing us the luxury of being able to devote time to this project; and all the student, novice and experienced researchers we have had the pleasure and honour to have known. Each one of them has influenced us and helped shape the researchers we each have become.

We would like to especially acknowledge Anne-Marie Morrissey, Louise Greenstock and Karen Stagnetti, three talented researchers who allowed us the privilege of sharing their research experiences in detail.

We are grateful for the ongoing support and encouragement from the team at Sage, in particular Katie Metzler and Anna Horvai. We thank them for their patience and insistence that we continue on our own journey of sharing our knowledge with others.

1

WHY BECOME INVOLVED IN RESEARCH IN EARLY CHILDHOOD?

This introductory chapter outlines the context and importance of research in the early childhood field. It introduces the early childhood landscape, providing an historical account of how it has been positioned and what has been privileged. This provides the context within which the challenges specific to early childhood research are located. The sensitivities surrounding researching with young children in early childhood settings are acknowledged as needing thoughtful consideration in the research design and research process.

Key chapter questions are:

- Why research?
- What do I need to understand about the nature of research?
- Why research in early childhood?
- What do I need to know about the early childhood field so that I can understand the current context?
- How have children been viewed?
- What are some of the complexities surrounding research with young children?

While this book draws from a range of research experiences, from novice to more experienced researchers, this chapter specifically introduces two student researchers, Amy and Lara, whose research journeys we follow throughout the book. Their research journeys, along with all the other examples, provide more practical insights into the world of research in early childhood. The experiences of all researchers who have contributed their research stories to this book demonstrate that research perhaps is not as straightforward as one might think, yet can be very rewarding not only for the researcher but also for the early childhood field.

WHY RESEARCH?

There are a number of reasons why people engage in research. Often it is because they are obliged to as a requirement of a course or to meet certain job criteria. There are, on the other hand, others who feel a deep commitment to explore and investigate issues to inform practice or to shape policy, and in their jobs have the capacity to undertake such research. When you mention the term 'research', you will find that it draws different reactions from different groups of people. Undergraduate students often fear research units in their courses, considering them difficult, complex, and something that is beyond their realms of understanding. 'It's like another language' was how one undergraduate student described her initial engagement in the research process. Some may view research as daunting to begin with, while those who are more experienced researchers, or who can see the potential of the impact on practice that research can have, tend to see it as exciting, rewarding and worthwhile. Whichever view you now hold, we hope that by engaging with this book and the experiences and journeys of the researchers' who have so willingly shared their experiences within the book, you will gain an understanding of the importance of research and the impact it can have on the lives of others as well as your own.

Research offers an opportunity to examine practice, to search for knowledge, to satisfy curiosity, to prove or disprove a theory or hypothesis. 'More and more we need high quality research to promote new knowledge because the world is ever changing. This provides a sound knowledge base upon which to respond to change' (Aubrey, David, Godfrey, & Thompson, 2000, p. 6). It is rightly perceived as a carefully planned, systematic investigation of an issue, incident, experience, trend, event, or fact, usually conducted to find out further information or to improve a situation. Being involved in empirical research, research that gains knowledge by direct or indirect observation, experience or experiments, enables the researcher to collect data about people and contexts using a range of methods and to consider the impact of such data. Engaging in pure research (basic, fundamental research) advances fundamental knowledge about the human world supporting or refuting theories. This is where a general explanation is developed relating to an issue or situation, establishing cause-and-effect relationships between variables. It will be for others to explicate the usefulness of the theory for practice, thereby translating your research into practice. When research is in the social sciences, concerned with society and human behaviours, it becomes more complex as it impacts on the lived experiences of the participants either directly or indirectly, which calls for close attention to the ethical issues this raises. There is no question that research is a complex process, and at times problematic, which 'demands the ability to be both reflective and reflexive' (Aubrey et al., 2000, p. 5). Researchers experience many issues that need careful consideration to ensure their research is not only conducted in an ethical way, employing appropriate methods to obtain the data, but that the findings are sound and can lead to change or the confirmation or expansion of knowledge.

WHAT DO I NEED TO UNDERSTAND ABOUT THE NATURE OF RESEARCH?

'Those who are more experienced know that research is often tedious, painfully slow, and rarely spectacular. They realize that the search for truth and the solution of important problems take a great deal of time and energy and the intensive application of logical thinking' (Best & Kahn, 2006, p. 28). In reality the research process is often not as streamlined or straightforward as appears in books. A research professor once advised 'research is often rather messy and you need to keep this in mind, believing it will all make sense in the end'. There is a 'messiness' about research as things are not always clear at the start and only develop clarity as the research process continues and becomes more refined. Things are rarely black and white and easily definable. As Walford (2001) suggests, 'the real world of research is one of constraint and compromise' (p. 5). However, by working through the research process you have the potential to make an impact at some level with the eventual findings.

In order to help you better comprehend some of the 'messiness' and complexities of research in general, and researching in early childhood specifically, we, the authors, have drawn on our own experiences and the experiences of others in an effort to provide true to life examples. These glimpses of research in action are drawn from the education, health and community services sectors due to the interdisciplinary and holistic nature of early childhood. They concentrate on research undertaken with young children or issues related to early childhood. The research examples also represent different types of research, methodologically and in capacity and purpose, from an undergraduate honours thesis to large-scale research projects run by teams of researchers. These research projects are drawn from different countries of the world, with a concentration on Australia and the United Kingdom. What should be clear to you by the end of the book is that every research project is unique, with differing demands placed on the researcher. It is reassuring to think, however, that there is a process which you can follow for undertaking research, so by thinking through the design of your research project will in fact give you some clarity on where your research is heading.

WHY RESEARCH IN EARLY CHILDHOOD?

As we move along in the twenty-first century there is a strong emphasis emerging all over the world in policy documents and government initiatives for evidence-informed practice, none more so than in the early childhood field. For example, in Australia, the Council of Australian Governments (COAG) (2006) nominated four priority areas for Australia as part of the Australian Government's National Reform Agenda in terms of building its human capital. Of the four areas, one focuses directly on high-quality early childhood programs to promote the wellbeing and development of Australia's children. In response to this policy reform, all Australian governments agreed to explore ways in which more can be done to provide children with the best possible start in life. Building a strong platform for healthy development and effective learning in the early years is linked with the provision of nurturing and responsive quality experiences and programs. Early childhood is in the spotlight and as such there are many opportunities for research in this area to inform policy and practice.

The importance of a young child's early years cannot be overstated as the research evidence concludes that the early stages of life lay the foundation for all future development. The ramifications of this is that action will make a difference in these significant years as long as it is targeted, well designed and thoughtfully executed (McCain & Mustard, 1999; Schonkoff & Phillips, 2000). This is where research can play a vital role, as actions can only be successfully tailored if informed by evidence, and this evidence comes from sound research. With new research relating to teaching and learning, and innovative projects in Australia and other countries, we see the expansion of the professional knowledge base related to quality practice in early childhood. For example, in Australia, there is a questioning of beliefs that have underpinned curriculum production and early childhood advice for at least the last 40 years. The ramification of these changing times is that early childhood policy makers and practitioners need to be prepared to rethink the field and their own professional activities, exploring the origins, sustainment, and changes in attitudes and practices over time and how current processes are linked to the construction of good practice from an informed point of view. Without the use of information-gathering critique incorporating the range and variety of needs and responses, early childhood education and care 'can only foster dominant perspectives; the field thus functions to silence the voices of diverse others' (Cannella, 1997, p. 17).

Research can act to expand definitions of what constitutes quality practice. For example, when taking a holistic approach to early childhood, research can advise the formation of cross-portfolio, inter-sectorial and interdisciplinary partnerships that can make a difference in young children's and families' lives. This linking of services is reflected in the evidence that calls for new ways of working across the Children's Services sector boundaries that exist between education, care, welfare and health services, ensuring that practice is inclusive of all children and families (Siemon, 2002, p. 2). It is suggested that universal, secondary and statutory service responses need to form more unified service systems where each level of service builds on the strengths of the others in order to address increasingly complex needs. Therefore, current government reforms require new and consistent policy and practice agendas, focusing on children's wellbeing, education and care. These need to be informed by research.

WHAT DO I NEED TO KNOW ABOUT THE EARLY CHILDHOOD FIELD SO THAT I CAN UNDERSTAND THE CURRENT CONTEXT?

The early childhood field has been described as diverse and multidisciplinary, which has grown from a long tradition of care and education. The very act of defining the early childhood field becomes quite problematic when you consider the diverse settings that young children and their families attend, the multidisciplinary nature of the field, as well as the age range of children served (birth to eight years being the internationally recognised early childhood period). There are complex layers and connections between government and non-government organisations led by voluntary and religious groups, education systems involving government, independent, Catholic and other religious schools, community organisations, free-market forces, small business owner-operators and health systems. If we take Australia as an example, we see how separate histories and traditions of early childhood 'care' programs and 'education' programs have resulted in substantially different goals, purposes and practices in childcare, preschools, kindergartens and nurseries. These differences have been reinforced by policy, funding and administrative divisions within and between the sectors and at the government and local levels.

Countries differ as to the history of their early childhood services, and so you will be well placed if you spend time trying to gain a sense of this history and how the sector has been positioned over time, thereby acquiring an understanding of the subtleties that may impact on your research. In Australia, 'education and care has evolved in a somewhat haphazard way in response to varying community needs within changing ideological and socio-political environments' (Elliott, 2006, p. 2). This has manifested into a care–education dichotomy in the early childhood field, and the inability of policy and professional groups to transcend the care–education distinctions has resulted in a two-tiered system of early childhood education and early childhood care. What this means is that there are different requirements as to staff qualifications and professional standards, different regulations and licensing processes, resulting in differing levels of pay, resource provision and working conditions for staff. Yet, despite this, Australian early childhood education and care services are generally considered to be well developed and well established by international standards. It is this type of background information that helps you, as a researcher, contextualise the current context you are experiencing.

HOW HAVE CHILDREN BEEN VIEWED?

The modern notion of childhood came into existence as a consequence of the creation of the nation state and the rise of capitalism (Prout, 2005). Political, economic, technological, social and cultural changes paved the way for new social and cultural possibilities as people were freed from old forms of social control. Traditional religious beliefs were challenged, which created conditions for rationalist and individualist ideas and values. Played out over time and shaped by different circumstances, the modern idea of childhood transpired. During the eighteenth and nineteenth centuries, a dominant image of childhood was universalised with the introduction of mass schooling and new laws that sought to provide children with greater protection. This resulted in a more sentimental view of children that emphasised their innocence and vulnerability (Prout, 2005). The institution of childhood was further questioned with the rise of feminism and other social movement in the 1970s and 1980s (Johnny, 2006). By the mid-twentieth century all children were thought to be entitled to certain common elements and rights of childhood and were seen as competent.

The early childhood sector also has a history of different images and beliefs about children and the way that children learn and develop. What is certain is that this 'history of childhood', along with other factors concerning the way society conceptualises infants and young children, influences how early childhood and young children are defined. As someone researching in the early childhood field, understanding the perspectives of others, related to the nature of children, will help you appreciate why there could be issues around access, participation and the protection of young children.

WHAT ARE SOME OF THE COMPLEXITIES SURROUNDING RESEARCH WITH YOUNG CHILDREN?

With children now being acknowledged as capable and competent, having agency and rights, there is more widespread acceptance of the importance of involving young children in research that relates to their own lives. The form that this involvement takes can vary, such as a shift from children being the object of research, to actively participating in the research process itself. In one study, which focused on childhood wellbeing – How to grow up happy – Thoilliez (2011) positioned the child participants as 'interlocutors' able to 'contribute to conceptualizing what a child would need in order to be happy' (p. 328). This is based on the notion that young children are able to give their opinions about issues that impact on their lives, and that they have a right to do so. As Jover and Thoilliez (2011) acknowledge, 'children have rights, and not just rights to protection, but also the right to express themselves and be heard on matters concerning them' (p. 128). Lundy (2007) proposes that four elements need to be present – space, voice, audience and influence – for children to have both the right to express a view and the right to have their views given due weight. It is argued that it is not common for all four elements to be present in the research, with the latter two elements often missing. These elements are defined as:

- Space – children must be given the opportunity to express a view;
- Voice – children must be facilitated to express their views;
- Audience – the view must be listened to;
- Influence – the view must be acted upon, as appropriate.

Thought needs to be given to how children and their views are represented within the research, how data are interpreted, who is involved in this process, and the power dynamics and status that already exist between adults and children. We need to be reflective about the assumptions we draw relating to children's perspectives, interests and attitudes (Mayall, 2002). We need to be mindful that our position as an adult implies superior knowledge. This means that methodological approaches and ethical considerations need deliberation. When considering methodological approaches the researcher must choose strategies which allow children to feel comfortable and confident in what is required of them, and draw on young children's communication strengths. Incorporating multi-modal means of communication, such as drawing, taking photographs and conversing with children about their experiences, enables researchers to gain a more comprehensive view and better represent children's understandings. As Mayall (2002, p. 121) states 'good information about childhood must start from children's experience'. Ethical issues revolve around access, the notion of informed consent, ownership, confidentiality, protection, and feedback. It has become a practice for some researchers whose research involves young children, to reflect on the research process itself and the power relationships between the researcher and the researched (Bolzan & Gale, 2011; Mayall, 2002) in an attempt to distribute the power base more equally. This means the adult researcher will need to relinquish the power, finding ways for children to realise that they have power. One way of achieving this is to take the position of a 'least adult role' (Corsaro & Molinari, 2000) where the researcher allows the children to lead the interactions. In this scenario, the children initiate contact, determining when the researcher is invited into their conversations or play, and decide the agenda. This means having conversations rather than interviewing children as they then have control and set the pace and the direction of the dialogue. The power dynamics certainly need careful consideration when research involves young children to ensure the integrity of the data and analysis. Researching with children also demands the researcher to be somewhat flexible and open to changing methods during the research process. Once children are positioned as collaborators in the research process, the researcher must be flexible enough to take up children's ideas about the research as it progresses.

Issues such as these will be unpacked further as you work your way through this book and read the experiences of other researchers. There are benefits to engaging children in research, such as building a positive sense of agency, enhanced social competence and relationships, critical thinking, metacognition and creativity (Fielding & Bragg, 2003). However, if committed to privileging children's voices in research, and acknowledging that they have rights in the research process which are equal to the rights of adult research participants, then thought must be given to how this can be accomplished in an ethical, responsive, respectful and effective way. Children are also members of families and communities. As researchers undertake projects with children they are often linking in with families. They may also find themselves focusing on particular issues pertinent to the adults in children's lives. Many of the considerations for researching with children should also be respected as researchers work with parents and within communities.

RESEARCH JOURNEYS: AMY AND LARA

A feature of this book is the research journeys of two doctoral research students, Amy and Lara. Their stories are woven throughout many of the chapters, illustrating how they dealt with different aspects of the research process, what they thought at the time, and how this impacted on what they did next. So while we dip in and out of the research projects and experiences of others in a somewhat eclectic way, we follow the complete journey of both Amy and Lara, charting the challenges and successes they experienced as they worked towards their doctoral qualification. Their accounts are reflective and frank in the hope that other student researchers can identify with them. First, we will introduce Amy, followed by Lara.

Amy was based in Australia and was extremely interested in exploring children's early gifted development. When she began her research Amy didn't have any 'fixed ideas' about what giftedness was. She saw IQ as just one of many indicators of what can be advanced thinking or development. Amy explains her interest in the topic as follows: 'It's just the whole issue, I suppose, of early intellectual development and what promotes it. I think gifted development is an interesting example of intellectual development that can perhaps teach us things about intellectual development across the whole population.' Amy followed this interest by looking at the pretend play development of a group of infants and toddlers, taking pretend play as a measure of their cognitive development, and the maternal interactions in that development and how they promoted children's play and thinking. Amy's thesis was entitled: 'Relationships between early pretence, mother–child interactions and later IQ: a longitudinal study of average to high ability children'. Her Abstract is included here to give you a sense of her research work, and to help you put her story as a researcher in context. Amy was invited to be featured in this book as she undertook a quantitative study, which went against the more qualitative approaches usually undertaken for the topic. Applying this approach challenged Amy in many ways, as you will read in the various chapters.

Amy's Abstract

Little is known about the early development of intellectually gifted or high ability children, and the role of caregiver interactions in that development. The aim of this study was to investigate relationships between early development and interactions, and later IQ. Participants were 21 mother–child dyads, many of whom were recruited on the basis of having a greater than usual likelihood of showing advanced development. Based on Piaget's theory on the cognitive implications of children's emerging pretence, pretend play development was selected as a measure of early development. Level and frequency of play were used as variables, based on Brown's (1997) Pretend Play Observation Scale. Mother–child interactions were examined for levels of stimulation and challenge, within the theoretical framework of Vygotsky's (1978) concept of the Zone of Proximal Development (ZPD) [Vygotsky, 1978], and the related construct of scaffolding. Interaction measures included level and frequency of maternal play modelling, and mothers' use of different types of verbal scaffolding, including categories of total verbal and play comment, and higher order categories of total higher order, didactic, analogical/transformational and metacognitive. Dyads were videotaped in monthly play sessions when children were aged from 8 to 17 months. Data analyses were based on three five-minute samples containing the child's highest level of play demonstrated within each age range of 8–9 months, 11–13 months, and 16–17 months. Children were assessed at 4.5–6 years on the Stanford-Binet Intelligence Scale (FE). Results showed that children's global IQ scores ranged from 96–150, with a mean of 123. Results for verbal and abstract-visual sub-scales were similar. Unexpectedly, the group as a whole demonstrated advanced levels of pretend play, with all children showing at least emerging pretence at 8–9 months, and most demonstrating pretend transformations by 11–13 months. All mothers modelled play levels in advance of age-typical expectations for children. A series of ANOVAs, based on higher (HGIQ) and lower (LGIQ) IQ groups, showed no significant relationships between play levels and global, verbal or abstract-visual IQ. A series of Mann-Whitney U-Tests were used to analyse data on child and mother play frequencies and maternal verbal scaffolding. At the 11–13 months session, HGIQ dyads showed higher frequencies of child play, and lower frequencies of maternal play modelling, than LGIQ dyads. This suggested faster learning by HGIQ children, and earlier transfer of responsibility for dyadic activity to children by HGIQ mothers. Mothers in the HGIQ dyads demonstrated more pretend transformations and engaged in more analogical/transformational utterances than mothers in LGIQ dyads, at the 8–9 months session. At the 11–13 months session, HGIQ mothers continued to demonstrate more frequent analogical/transformational verbal scaffolding, as well as significantly more metacognitive utterances than LGIQ mothers. The results provide evidence of advanced development in high ability children from the first year of life. The findings also support the notion that the caregivers of high ability children engage them in challenging and stimulating interactions from an early age. The findings of advanced play levels for the whole group are attributed to intensive maternal scaffolding, data analysis procedures, and the provision of supportive play materials.

Our second featured researcher in this book is Lara. Lara was based in the United Kingdom during her doctoral studies and her research started as a project that was to include two topics. One topic was the way that graphic symbols were used with young children aged 3–5 years in the classroom, and the other was the collaboration between staff in a Foundation Stage setting. (The Foundation Stage is the curriculum phase in England for children aged Birth to Five years. This study refers to Nursery and Reception age groups – children aged 3–5 years). The choice of the topic and setting were heavily influenced by Lara's work as a teaching assistant in schools in the United Kingdom with young children, and using graphic signs and symbols with these children. Lara was at the time looking to change jobs and identified a studentship which was a doctoral project that was going to be in an associated topic set locally. For Lara, it was a case of perfect timing for her to undertake higher degree research and be supported financially while she did. Lara's thesis was titled: 'An investigation exploring the experiences of a range of practitioners using graphic symbols with children in Foundation Stage (3–5 years) school settings'. Lara was invited to be featured in this book because she took a contrasting approach to that of Amy, and also because her research was part of a larger project, which again has different ramifications to other research projects undertaken by some students. Lara's Abstract follows so you can understand the significance of her research and its findings.

Lara's Abstract

The primary objective of the research was to explore practitioners' experiences of using graphic symbols with children in Foundation Stage (3–5 years) school settings. For the main study, 44 interviews were conducted with teachers, teaching assistants/nursery nurses and speech and language therapists. These were conducted face to face by the researcher and were all located within the East Midlands (UK). The findings of this research were developed as a framework of themes and subthemes. There were four major themes identified in the data and 15 subthemes, reflecting the major repeating ideas and patterns in the data. To further explain these themes and subthemes and 'tell the story' of the data set as a whole, a theoretical framework was developed. This theoretical framework encompasses two original theoretical constructs explaining the data, 'models of reasoning' and 'perceptions of professional roles'. These constructs explain the ways that practitioners referred to their experiences of thinking and reasoning about how to use symbols, as well as how they perceived their own role in the implementation of symbols and the roles of other practitioners they worked with. Particular attention was paid to their experiences of collaborative working when using symbols and the findings suggest that professional roles are sometimes unclear and that opportunities to communicate with other practitioners are not always consistently available. The research demonstrated that the use of symbols in Foundation Stage school settings is common among special and mainstream provision and that symbols are used for a wide variety of purposes with children with a wide range of needs.

USING THIS BOOK

We would encourage you to use this book as a compass point – take what is relevant to you and your research, and from time to time use the book to check your bearings. It is not designed to be prescriptive, but rather as a text you can dip in and out of depending on where you are in your own research journey. It is hoped that you will find something of value within the chapters to assist you with your research. Each chapter is structured around questions which one could ask relating to the chapter topic, with each chapter concluding with reflective questions for you to ponder in relation to your research project. We wish you well on your research journey!

2 ORIENTATION: 'IT'S LIKE ANOTHER LANGUAGE'

This chapter orientates readers to the research process, including an explanation about how epistemology, theoretical perspectives and methodology link together. It defines relevant terminology and considers philosophies relevant to research in and about early childhood. Lara shares some of her thoughts on beginning her research, and Amy outlines her orientation to her research project.

Key chapter questions are:

- What is epistemology?
- What is a theoretical perspective?
- What is a methodology?
- How do they link together?

Beginning research can be an exciting but also a daunting process. While you may be curious about the topic you are investigating, this excitement is often tempered with a sense of being overcome by the processes involved in undertaking the research. How do you know what you need to know when you do not know what you need to know? It can be quite overwhelming when you are trying to decide where and how to start researching, what the processes are, and the meaning of the words that other, more experienced researchers, are using when they are trying to explain things to you. The terminology used in research can at first appear like another language. There are some terms that are very specific to research processes and other words that have dual meanings – one of which is very specific to the research activities. Words like epistemology, theoretical perspective, methodology, qualitative and quantitative methods, to list a few, are significant to the research process as research is as much about being an abstract activity as it is about the pragmatic processes. This chapter will give you a basic understanding of some of the language and concepts used to describe research processes and practices. To begin this chapter, Lara shares some of her thoughts on how she felt about beginning her research.

> I was very new to the idea of creating new knowledge when I first started my doctoral studies. I spent a fair amount of time worrying about what 'original research' actually meant, until I read a seminal research methods book which explained that originality need not be as ground-breaking, as I feared. Having got over that initial hurdle, I began to consider what it meant to generate new knowledge and that is when I began to explore my epistemological approach. I read extensively on this which did help, but ultimately I would recommend undertaking training on this and speaking to supervisors and other mentors, until you find someone who can make it make sense for you.

Lara's suggestion of speaking to others who know a lot about the theoretical perspective or the research approaches that you are interested in is good advice and has been echoed particularly in our conversations with other novice researchers. For example, Maria is a doctoral student who is undertaking research using narrative methodology. You will read about her work in this chapter. Maria went to a week of master classes about narrative methodology. She says she felt she learnt more in that week talking to others than she had previously just reading about the methodology. Therefore, Lara's suggestion of undertaking training makes sense for anyone thinking about beginning the research process.

Novice researcher Rhys, was undertaking an introductory course about research methods in which he was being introduced to the research process and the different types of approach researchers took to gather evidence in order to answer their research questions. Rhys approached his first research task assignment with trepidation as nothing seemed to make sense and he could not see the links between all the different pieces of information his research methods lecturer was discussing about the value of research and how to undertake a research project. Each week the research methods lecturer addressed a different type of research methodology. In the beginning week, in the hour-long introductory presentation, the lecturer had 47 PowerPoint slides to try to capture the breadth of the research process. Rhys was so overwhelmed that he could not take anything in. The more lectures he went to the more confused he became about the research process. By week four of the course he was starting to think that understanding research was beyond him as he could not understand the terminology and he felt like the lecturer was speaking another language. He started to write down the words that the lecturer was using and grouped the words that were similar (Figure 2.1).

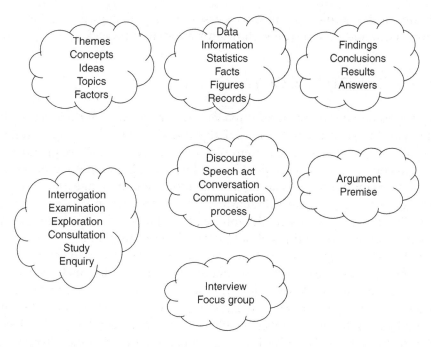

Figure 2.1   Understanding research

Slowly he was able to understand what the lecturer was trying to say and he was able to see the steps involved in a research investigation. Rhys began to comprehend how data was generated and how that data could be analysed and discussed, and conclusions drawn. Rhys was able to understand that there were multiple ways of undertaking research and each way had some variations on how the process was described.

There are many different ways in which individuals become more informed about research. Some people read extensively, others join a semester-long university class devoted to research processes, or find a set of intensive master classes. Whichever way you choose to gather the information to assist you to become a more skilful researcher, it is also really helpful to have a research mentor who can translate the terms and concepts into language that you understand. It can be very reassuring to know that there is someone who you can keep checking with to make sure that you have really understood the abstract ideas that surround the process, or the technical way in which some data gathering or data analysis is undertaken. In the first instance, it can be even more exciting to be part of a research team so that you have experienced others who model and scaffold research processes with you before you have to launch out and take responsibilities for a research project.

WHAT IS EPISTEMOLOGY?

Epistemology has a profound impact on the way you undertake research. It relates to the nature of the knowledge and the processes that created it. We all view the world in a certain way to make sense of it, so it is important to consider what is entailed in this knowing. Epistemology provides a platform for decisions relating to what kinds of knowledge are possible, adequate and legitimate (Maynard, 1994). Therefore, in order to clarify the direction of your research, you need to clarify your epistemological beliefs and understandings about knowledge production.

Crotty (1998) suggests that there are a number of epistemologies, naming the main ones as objectivism, constructionism and subjectivism. Objectivism is defined as viewing knowledge and meaning as existing apart from consciousness. This considers understandings and values to be objectified in the subjects of the study, which enables the researcher to uncover the objective truth. 'Reality is a physical and observable event' (Jones, Torres, & Arminio, 2006, p. 5). Constructivism is at the opposite end of the scale, in that knowledge and meaning are constructed through interactions with the world. 'There is no meaning without a mind. Meaning is not discovered, but constructed' (Crotty, 1998, p. 9). This process allows for different constructions of meaning from different people, not one true way. There is an interplay between the subject and the object to create the meaning. 'Reality is constructed through local human interaction' (Jones et al., 2006, p. 5). Subjectivism, however, positions things differently again, with meaning being ascribed to objects by subjects. This position is usually aligned with poststructuralist critical forms of research, where the emphasis is on enacting social change (transformation and emancipation) and challenging knowledge that is taken for granted. 'Reality is shaped by social, political, economic, and other values crystallized over time' (Jones et al., 2006, p. 5).

Researchers focusing on children, families and children's services need to be able to understand the relationship between a view of reality (ontology) – how the researcher views the world – and the meaning ascribed to knowledge and its creation (epistemology) – what is known or knowable in the world – in order to communicate the reasons underpinning the research design and methodology. Ontology is basically related to the study of the human condition or, as stated, the study of reality, whereas epistemology is considered to be the study of knowledge. These terms are important to the research process and will be mentioned frequently in readings and texts as you read more about the research process.

WHAT IS A THEORETICAL PERSPECTIVE?

Theoretical perspectives are shared frameworks of assumptions held within a discipline, sub-discipline or school of thought. They can be seen as a lens or belief system that guides the researcher in deciding what is worth investigating (knowing) and the purpose of research. The theoretical perspective reflects the epistemological and ontological stance of the researcher, however, can also be determined by the research topic. For example, investigations around social justice and equity benefit from taking a critical perspective so the power relations and empowerment can be focused upon. Theoretical perspectives are often described as the most influential frameworks informing research, as these assumptions shape the individual's thinking and approaches to gaining new knowledge.

It can be a little confusing for beginning researchers to discuss theoretical frameworks in relation to research. However, this helps to shape understandings and create the framework on which a research project can be structured. The theoretical framework is 'the philosophical stance that lies behind our chosen methodology' (Crotty, 1998, p. 7), which causes us to bring a set of assumptions to our methodology. These assumptions need to be identified and outlined and, in so doing, the theoretical framework is clarified. Theoretical perspectives shape all aspects of the research process. They guide the early childhood researcher in the way in which the research is conducted, and the conceptual approach and methodology. Furthermore, the literature explored in the process of the research is also influenced by the theoretical perspective. Theoretical perspectives are meant to be used as an analytic device that can help make sense of some major streams of thought, major lines of evidence and major areas of debate. Once a theoretical perspective is identified, this can be used to provide guidelines and principles about the way in which research should be conducted. Some of the possible theoretical perspectives that are considered in research, and are discussed in more detail in the following chapter, are:

- Positivist
- Interpretive
- Hermeneutics
- Critical
- Feminist

- Postcolonial
- Postmodernist
- Poststructuralist

Sometimes early childhood researchers find using these perspectives equally as confusing as other parts of the research process, even though they are meant to provide some structure and guidance. The terminology linked to each of the perspectives can be viewed as like another language to beginning researchers. It is therefore useful to understand the definitions for each of the perspectives, and this requires persistence and diligence on the part of the researcher.

The structure of the perspectives provides a logic with which a researcher can interrogate the data they have collected. This logic makes the interrogation valid and authentic. There needs to be a strong link between your epistemology and your theoretical perspective, as this will influence your choice of methodology and the methods you use to collect your data. There is a need for researchers to be reflexive thinkers as they go about developing the research project, thinking to and fro, as they create new knowledge and understandings about the potential of their research, and the perspective that underpins it.

Developing the theoretical perspective usually involves the following elements – identifying and defining concepts, exploring how they are linked, and then operationalising the concepts. These fours elements are sequentially linked together as shown in Figure 2.2.

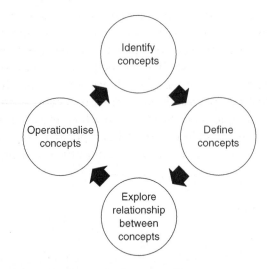

Figure 2.2   Clarifying the theoretical perspective

Having a theoretical framework is essential to ensuring some structure and reliability for the research process. Sonia saw herself as a very practical person and, in undertaking research with school-age care services for the local area government authority, resisted thinking about theoretical positions. Sonia made this decision as she thought her research work would appeal to the people that she was researching if it wasn't 'too theoretical'. School-age care services is an area that has had limited research so she was keen to gather the ideas and perspectives from as many of the stakeholders involved in the delivery of services as possible. In school-age child care services, she did lots of interviews with the adults and children. In addition, she took copious field notes about her visits to the services and she explored all the government policies and procedures and read the historical accounts of the development of the services. Sonia was swamped with data. The data included a range of interesting ideas and themes that she could pursue in more detail. She felt like she was an effective researcher because she had uncovered so much material. However, she had no idea how to then pull all these ideas together in a coherent way that would make her research project contribute new knowledge about the school-age child care sector. In some ways, she could see it as all new knowledge but there was no structure to the creation of the knowledge that would help others to see what she had found, and why she thought it was important. She had no theoretical position to help her sort and present the data in a coherent way. She had resisted thinking about a theoretical position because she thought that the qualitative data would tell its own story. She viewed a theoretical position as something very abstract and removed from the research process. Her credibility as a researcher was low because she could not coherently present her findings for the questions about school-age care that she was trying to answer.

The research process requires thinking about abstract ideas as the researcher takes the themes and concepts from the evidence and presents it in a different form. Sonia needed a theoretical framework if she was going to attract credibility as a scholar and present a solid research project. Sonia's research supervisor had to make her aware of how she could systematically think about her data and analyse it in ways that would be deemed credible and reliable by others. Using a theoretical position meant that Sonia could organise the data in coherent ways. Furthermore, others would be able to trace the conceptual thinking that underpinned the analysis and the thinking associated with the data. Once Sonia had been able to state the framework that surrounded her thinking and where the data fitted in the schema, it was easier for others to understand the relevance of her research. It made it seem more valid and reliable. Sonia was also happier as she found it easier to write about her research.

WHAT IS A METHODOLOGY?

Methodology is a term used to define the structured process of conducting research. It justifies and rationalises how the study should be undertaken. Answers to epistemological questions such as 'How do we know?', 'What does it mean to "know"?' and 'How is knowledge produced?' guide the selection of methodology, by defining the researcher's role in producing knowledge. There are many different methodologies used in various types of research. Research methodology is an embracing notion that is usually considered to include research design, data gathering and data analysis. Some possible methodologies are:

- Experimental research – a systematic approach in which the researcher manipulates one or more variables, and controls and measures any change in other variables;
- Action research – pursues action (or change) and research (or understanding) at the same time;
- Case study – is used to look at individuals, a small group of participants or a group, drawing conclusions only about that participant or group and only in that specific context;
- Ethnography – is the study of human social phenomena and communities;
- Phenomenological research – is the study of structures of experience or consciousness from the first-person point of view;
- Biography – explores the life of an individual;
- Grounded theory – develops a theory grounded in data from the field;
- Genealogy – reflects on current circumstances using descriptions of the interrelations of past practice and knowledge, throwing current rules into doubt;
- Narrative inquiry – is a way of thinking about and studying experience. Narrative inquiry follows a recursive, reflexive process of moving from the field (with starting points in telling or living of stories) to field texts (data) to interim research and final research texts;
- Discourse analysis – is in-depth, critical analysis of the social relations within data texts.

More about the specific features of some of these research methodologies will be discussed in chapters that follow.

HOW DO THEY LINK TOGETHER?

One of the most difficult parts of the research process is getting the right fit between the concepts to be examined, the perspectives to guide the research process and the methodologies and methods that will best uncover the appropriate data to answer the research questions. Now we would like to refer to Maria's story that we mentioned earlier in this chapter. The following example is taken from a conversation with Maria about her research and how she felt about engaging in research with children. Maria was interested in the way in which children and adults converse. Maria taught early childhood educators in a university setting and was particularly interested in how and 'why' adults engaged in conversations with children and what impact this had on children's wellbeing. She thought that if she knew more she would be able to teach adults to be better at listening and talking with children. Initially, in developing her research proposal, she was going to use the stories of adults who worked with children to present their perspective. She was going to use narrative inquiry as her research methodology. However, the more she thought about her proposal the more uncomfortable she felt that something was not quite right about the links between her theoretical perspective, her data collection methods and her own beliefs, which positioned children as having the right to participation. In consultation with her supervisors, she decided to expand her research to include the stories from children about how they engaged in conversation with adults. The theoretical perspective had an emphasis on the voices of children; however, it was these voices that were missing from her methodology and methods. By realising this, Maria was able to add to her research design and incorporate the stories of children, allowing her to examine the possible impact of the conversations between children and adults from both adults' and children's perspectives.

What is interesting about Maria's research is that she chose to privilege the voices of children. By working in this way she was true to how she positioned children as being capable and confident and informed about their own lives. Children are often very aware and curious about their circumstances and they are 'typically surrounded by multiple goals and expectations, including of their own early childhoods' (Woodhead, 2006). In their childhood, they engage in numerous roles and identities as they become involved in multiple relationships, activities and transitions. Moreover, children may experience separation, disruption, challenges and discontinuities. It makes sense when researching with children and about children to consider their perspectives on their own unique childhood. Woodhead (2006) argues that this research is a crucial starting point for policy and practice for early childhood services to help adults understand the children's needs and interests. However, there must be an alignment between theoretical perspectives, methodology and methods to allow for this to occur.

In early childhood both quantitative and qualitative methodologies have their place. Obviously, because work in this field is very much tied to relationships between professionals, children and their families, qualitative approaches are often chosen as these approaches deal more with the stories of individuals. However, quantitative approaches serve a significant purpose when trying to gain statistical information to support arguments, such as the rate at which children are progressing in developmental areas, the success of interventions, or how many families are coping with the stresses of everyday life. Such statistics can assist in determining the needs of children and families and in directing programs to address those needs. In the end, it is important not to demonise either approach as both can contribute to research in the field. Moreover, both approaches can be scientific in the broadest sense of the word and both can add value to the knowledge base in early childhood. Additionally, the ability to work with both approaches is a skill that will benefit the early childhood researcher, as this ability will enhance possibilities for high-quality research to take place and for the best method to be chosen at each juncture.

Amy has something to say about her orientation to research projects. In the following excerpt she provides a glimpse into her thinking about quantitative and qualitative methodologies and their strengths and differences.

> My research pathway was straight into quantitative research so I never thought too much about other approaches, my epistemological beliefs, etc. in approaching my thesis. I knew that my research pathway was quantitative/empirical. However, I have thought about other methodologies since. I now see all approaches as having value. I don't know if I am a positivist in the sense that I don't believe any approach is about the truth; to me, all research approaches have a truth to them. I see quantitative methods as being grounded in statistical probability, and that this lends a validity and persuasiveness to their findings. On the other hand, I know that there are a lot of other truths that quantitative research cannot account for. It is important to remember that a quantitative approach is just one tool in the research toolbox, albeit a very useful one and a widely accepted one.

Amy's research journey is an indication that there is much to be gained from considering multiple perspectives. She has become aware that there is no one way to do research and this will hold her in good stead as she progresses through her research career.

Launching into the research process is an exciting venture. Even though it may seem as though 'it's like another language' at first, give yourself time to become more immersed in the process. You will gain confidence in your abilities as a researcher as long as you take time to explore the possible links between your epistemological beliefs, theoretical perspectives, methodologies and methods.

REFLECTION POINTS

Use the following questions to assist you with orientating your research:

- What epistemological understandings do I bring to my research?
- What theoretical perspective do I feel most aligned with and why?
- How will this stance influence my choice of methodology?
- Which research methodologies am I curious about and want to find out more about?
- Does there seem to be a logical link between what I want to research and my plan of action?

☐ Summary

This chapter has attempted to help you to decipher some of the terminology and features of the research process. Hopefully you are feeling more confident about some of these features and the decision-making that is involved. These features include:

- understanding terminology like epistemology, theoretical perspectives and methodologies;
- how these concepts are linked in research projects.

---

3 EXPLORING AND THEORISING PERSPECTIVES

This chapter's main focus is on theoretical perspectives that guide the research process. The chapter details positivist, interpretive, hermeneutical, critical, feminist, postcolonial, postmodern and poststructuralist approaches, describing what each looks like. Also summarised is Foucauldian theory and how this can be applied in early childhood research. A discussion relating to how some of these approaches are changing the early childhood research landscape and why they are vital in renewing the way research and practice is approached is included. We hear from Lara about how she decided on the theoretical perspective for her study, and we also meet Sarah, a doctoral student, and hear about her research journey as she grapples with taking a more critical perspective for her research.

Key chapter questions are:

- How do I decide what is the best approach for my research?

  ○ Positivism
  ○ Interpretivism
  ○ Hermeneutics
  ○ Critical theory
  ○ Reconceptualised critical theory
  ○ Feminism
  ○ Postcolonialism
  ○ Postmodernism
  ○ Poststructuralism

- How are some of these approaches changing the early childhood research landscape?
- What does this mean for early childhood practice?

HOW DO I DECIDE WHAT IS THE BEST APPROACH FOR MY RESEARCH?

Your theoretical approach to your research guides all aspects of the research. It drives the way in which the research is conducted, the methodological tools used and the theory and literature that is explored. Deciding which approach you will use for your research is perhaps the most difficult research decision you will make. It can be more difficult than deciding on a research topic. Research topics are often made up of issues we are extremely passionate about and this makes the decision of what to study somewhat more straightforward than deciding how you will study it.

Sometimes decisions are made because a particular theoretical perspective seems to stand out as suiting the research question or questions you may be trying to answer. Your research approach may well be decided for you as you join a team which has already conceptualised the direction of a project. At other times questions about research design are solved by pragmatic issues such as timing and spatial location. In order to make an informed decision about which theoretical perspective to use for your research, consider the following questions:

- What does each perspective represent?
- What are the constraints of each perspective?
- What are the enablers?
- Does the perspective chosen suit the research question or questions, the research context, the research population and the timing?

To begin to explore these questions it is necessary to understand what each perspective stands for. Therefore, this next section will detail the characteristics of positivism, interpretivism, hermeneutics, critical theory, reconceptualised critical theory, feminism, postcolonialism, postmodernism, and poststructuralism, so that this significant research choice may be made somewhat easier. Each perspective is detailed below.

Positivism

According to Ponterotto (2005) positivism, a form of philosophical realism, relies heavily on the hypothetico-deductive method. This scientific method requires:

> systematic observation and description of phenomena contextualised within a model or theory, the presentation of hypotheses, the execution of tightly controlled experimental study, the use of inferential statistics to test hypotheses, and

... the interpretation of the statistical results in light of the original theory. (Ponterotto, 2005, p. 128)

Positivism was part of the modernist era and dates back to the nineteenth century. It has been the dominant force in science for over 150 years, where proponents believe that reality can be 'captured and understood' (Denzin & Lincoln, 2011, p. 8). If you are to undertake a positivist approach to research, then your research is based on theory verification. You will begin with a set hypothesis that you are seeking to prove and will be interested in cause-and-effect phenomena that can be studied, verified and generalised (Ponterotto, 2005). You will see yourself as an objective researcher and you will need to develop various techniques in your research that adhere to the rules of reliability and validity. You will be seeking scientific 'truth' through objective study and will remain the detached researcher in order to maintain objectivity.

This notion that there can be one absolutely true answer to any research question has proved a point of great contention even among positivists. As such, postpositivism arose out of dissatisfaction with this notion (Ponterotto, 2005). Postpositivists believe that one 'true' reality cannot be captured and so those who adhere to this perspective are more concerned with theory falsification than with theory verification (Ponterotto, 2005). To demonstrate such understanding, Ponterotto (2005) concurs with Guba and Lincoln (1994) who state that while the presence of one million white swans cannot confidently verify the notion that all swans are white, the presence of one black swan can disprove such a theory. Despite their differences, however, both positivists and postpositivists seek explanations that lead to the prediction and control of phenomena and both act as the foundation for quantitative research (Ponterotto, 2005).

In early childhood, positivist, postpositivist and quantitative approaches in general have their place and are frequently used. Governments and larger organisations often use such approaches, or a blend of quantitative and qualitative approaches, particularly in larger studies. Australian examples include the federal government's Family Support program and the Australian Early Development Index (AEDI). Additionally, programs such as Sure Start in the UK would adopt similar approaches.

Positivist research is highly valued as a scientific approach and thus holds weight in the research community. This approach is useful when short, sharp studies are necessary, where pragmatic questions need to be answered and when statistical information is needed to substantiate and add value to an argument. A positivist approach can be a very direct and functional way to gain useful information that can be used to create arguments about what practices are most helpful in particular situations, what aspects of practice or programs need greater attention and what types of program should be delivered.

Interpretivism

Interpretive theory explores the complex world of lived experience from the point of view of those who live it (Schwandt, 2000). This theory assumes that reality is a social construction and it is the researcher through whom reality is revealed (Diaz-Andrade, 2009). In interpretive research, both the researcher and the participants, and the interactions between the two, work to construct the social world (Diaz-Andrade, 2009). Interpretivists understand that the interpretations of the researcher and the research participants impact on how the research comes to be understood and examined. Thus, interpretivists seek to find meaning in human action (Schwandt, 2000).

According to Ponterotto (2005) interpretivism and constructivism (as an epistemology) are closely related. Interpretivist and constructivist researchers work with the notion that meaning is hidden and that it is deep reflection that occurs through the dialogue between researcher and participant that assists in making meaning more visible (Ponterotto, 2005). As the terms suggest, the researcher and participant co-construct and interpret meaning through the dialogue they engage in throughout the research process (Diaz-Andrade, 2009; Ponterotto, 2005). Ponterotto (2005) states that this perspective can be traced back to Immanuel Kant (1966 [1781]), who believed that an objective reality cannot be separated from the participant, who interprets the reality from his/her own perspective. Thus, the participant constructs the reality and so it is not an objective reality. This does not mean that the process is not authentic, but that quality arguments rather than statistics are the focus (Diaz-Andrade, 2009).

Hermeneutics

Hermeneutic inquiry focuses on the notion of interpretation. Hermeneutic researchers try to make sense of data in ways that allow new understandings to emerge (Denzin & Lincoln, 2000). Hermeneutic researchers attest to the fact that there is only interpretation and that even perception is part of the interpretation process (Denzin & Lincoln, 2000). The main argument in this perspective is that nothing is value-free and so there is no such thing as an objective researcher.

Hermeneutic researchers understand that interpretation is often a result of language. In this vein, Hans-Georg Gadamer (2006) stated that understanding is impacted on by conversation, in that what we might say is influenced by the way we converse with others and the way in which language and understanding might grow out of conversation. Therefore, neither language nor conversation is value-free, as these notions are always subject to interpretation by both the speaker and the listener.

Hermeneutic researchers argue that nothing or no one can claim a privileged position. When engaging in qualitative inquiry these researchers utilise a hermeneutic circle where everything is viewed and understood in relation to everything else. In this sense, the whole is seen in terms of the part and the part in terms of the whole (Smith, 2007). It is argued that understanding can never fully be gained as the process is continuous and circular. However, the real skill in this tradition comes from deciding when sufficient understanding has been gained from the process, resulting in the researcher exiting the circle at that point to report on the findings.

What hermeneutics brings to the research process is the acknowledgement that understanding is blinkered and that interpretation is always undertaken within certain boundaries (Denzin & Lincoln, 2000). Denzin & Lincoln (2000, p. 286) attest that despite these restrictions hermeneutical researchers can:

> ...transcend the inadequacies of thin descriptions of decontextualised facts and produce thick descriptions of social texts characterised by the contexts of their production, the intentions of their producers and the meanings mobilised in the process of their construction.

Thus, it is this very attention to detail, context and language that allows hermeneutic researchers to bring richness to the qualitative process and to the understandings that arise from their research.

Critical theory

Critical theorists are interested in creating a more egalitarian and democratic society. The origins of Critical theory were with the Frankfurt School in the Institute of Social Research at the University of Frankfurt in the 1920s (Ponterotto, 2005). These Critical theorists were influenced by the work of Marx, Kant, Hegel and Weber. This means that Critical theorists are concerned with power and oppression, believing that the lived experience is socially constructed and mediated through power relations.

Critical theorists adhere to the ideological argument that draws on structuralist theory to argue that social services like education are part of an ideological state apparatus (Althusser, 1971). Such thought is underpinned by the notion that the promise of democracy in late capitalist society is necessarily flawed as the 'state' will hold the ultimate power and that power will not always work in the interests of true social democracy, despite the appearance of neutrality or social democratic rhetoric (Macfarlane, 2006).

While there is no single critical theory there are certain basic tenets that assist us to understand how the theory works. First, Critical theory is a form of social and cultural criticism, which implies that all thought is 'fundamentally mediated by power relations' (Ponterotto, 2005, p. 130). Additionally, Critical theorists believe that facts can never be separated from beliefs, values or ideology; that language is central to subjectivity; that oppression exists in many forms and is part of many interconnections; and, that mainstream research practices actually reproduce oppression in relation to class, race and gender (Ponterotto, 2005).

Critical theory often presents a point of contention for researchers. The type of Critical theory that we have just discussed here is what is referred to as big 'C' critical theory or Critical-ideological theory (Ponterotto, 2005). This type of Critical theory deals with power as a repressive force that is imposed largely by state apparatuses. It is this particular understanding of power that differentiates Critical-ideological theory from versions of critical theory that understand power in other ways and thus have a more postmodern approach.

This form of Critical theory sits well within the early childhood field in many respects. As some of the research in early childhood includes work related to vulnerable children and families, it is easy to take the view that such families may be suffering oppression. Indeed, it is not difficult to see such oppression in our world. Additionally, the more romantic and nostalgic (Jenks, 1996) images of childhood that have long permeated the early childhood psyche lay the foundation for the transformational characteristics of Critical theory and its use in research. It would be fair to say that this theory has dominated research work in this area in past decades.

Reconceptualised critical theory

It is important to note that, as previously mentioned, there is no one type of critical theory. Indeed, many critical theorists would argue with what has been stated above. Moreover, at the beginning of the twenty-first century, critical theory has been reconceptualised to become what is known as a critical social theory. This reconceptualisation situates critical theory as concerned with:

> ...issues of power and justice and the ways that the economy, matters of race, class and gender, ideologies, discourses, education, religion and other social institutions and cultural dynamics interact to construct a social system. (Kinchloe & McLaren, 2000, p. 281)

This reconceptualisation of critical theory has moved away from notions of emancipation and on to alternative conceptualisation of power, subtlety, ambiguity and functions of discourse (Kinchloe & McLaren, 2000). There is now a focus on the ways in which power operates to shape thought and consciousness and thus, oppression (Kinchloe & McLaren, 2000). This shift in thinking has coincided with the rise of postmodernism.

Feminism

Feminist researchers challenge the notion that 'common-sense' thinking produces natural understandings about gender (Wheedon, 1997). Feminist researchers seek to transform the role of women by unpacking taken-for-granted understandings about women (Olesen, 2000). Where many individuals may consider it 'natural' for women to take on nurturing roles and for men to take on more aggressive roles, feminist theory provides us with a different take on this notion of 'naturalness'. Feminists are more likely to take as a starting point 'the patriarchal structure of society' (Wheedon, 1997, p. 1) and will examine the impact of this structure on women and their opportunities for success. Wheedon (1997) defines the term 'patriarchal' as referring to the power relations in society where women's interests are subordinate to men's interests. Such power relations can take many forms, which are not always structural. Rather, these power relations are understood in terms of the social role of women being defined in terms of men (Wheedon, 1997). Additionally, feminist theory seeks to examine oppression, primarily the oppression of women, but also to understand the reasons people oppress each other.

Both Wheedon (1997) and Tong (1989) state that there are several types of feminist theory. These authors list the types as liberal, Marxist, radical, socialist, postmodern and poststructuralist. As in the case of other perspectives mentioned in this chapter, there is no one way to understand feminist theory. In fact, each of the aforementioned feminist theories has a different approach to understanding the issues of patriarchy. The different traditions in feminist research mean that many perspectives abound and therefore contestation occurs even among feminists. Feminist research is diverse and uses a wide range of methods, all the time seeking to work within and against (Lather, 1996) taken-for-granted understandings about gender, patriarchy, oppression and power.

Postcolonialism

It is argued that there are two contemporary interpretations of the word 'postcolonial' (Viruru & Cannella, 2001). The first interpretation is indicative of some concern as it implies that the addition of the prefix 'post' indicates that the period of colonialism is over. The second interpretation indicates the end of the period where indigenous people are appropriated from their lands but acknowledges the continuation of the effects of colonisation 'through discursive practices and philosophical domination' (Viruru & Cannella, 2001, p. 158). What this situation highlights is that the discussion that takes place between these two views can illuminate dominant narratives, which work to emphasise current power structures. In short, such discussion can continue to objectify individuals as the 'Other'.

In the postmodern tradition, postcolonial researchers are concerned with issues surrounding discourse, power, oppression, agency, representation, identity and history (Viruru & Cannella, 2001). According to Viruru and Cannella (2001, p. 161):

> Colonisation produces a 'subject people' ... by creating knowledge about the people through surveillance. Authority is created over the subject peoples through the construction of two stereotyped groups, as if in opposition to each other. One group becomes the oppressed, the other the oppressor.

Postcolonial researchers are interested in human contexts with respect to the social, cultural and economic conditions within which individuals live. Moreover, postcolonial theorists do not call for violent resistance but will focus on discourse as a site of 'contestation and freedom' (Dhillon, 1999, p. 194). Additionally, postcolonial researchers are more likely to work within Western academic discourse (Dhillon, 1999) and also work within and against (Lather, 1996; Macfarlane, 2006) Western understanding. These researchers seek to highlight how individuals are 'othered' and how such processes lead to exclusive practices.

Postmodernism

Most researchers think of the postmodern period as a period that 'came of age' around the end of the twentieth century. It was thought that the term was first conceptualised by Bell in 1973 and that later Touraine (1984) wrote about the notion that traditional secular beliefs and taken-for-granted categories of community membership no longer prevailed. However, the seminal work on postmodernism is considered to be *The Postmodern Condition* (Lyotard, 1984).

Postmodernists consider that current social conditions are discontinuous, uncertain, insecure and nostalgic (Jenks, 1996). The postmodern times that we live in are characterised by 'hyper-reality', that is, a society 'saturated with ever increasing forms of representation' (Kinchloe & McLaren, 2000, p. 292). It is this hyper-reality that contributes to the discontinuous and insecure nature of life as it is currently experienced. For example, it is often said that society is suffering from moral decay because life is 'just not what it used to be'. However, Jenks (1996) argues that the social changes that are currently and continuously being experienced are not indicative of moral decay but are simply a symptom of the postmodern condition (Lyotard, 1984).

Postmodernists challenge the notion of absolute or universal truth. These researchers also challenge understandings of fixed identities, believing instead that identities are multiple, complex and ever changing (Grieshaber & Cannella, 2001). These identities are also positioned in relation to particular discourses and to discursive practices (Grieshaber & Cannella, 2001).

It might be useful at this point to explore the notion of discourse. Discourse is the term used to name systems of language use, which are, at the same time, systems of power relations (Macfarlane, 2006). Discourses constitute the subjects – including human subjects – which they appear simply to describe. Discourses are systems for producing what is sayable rather than being the words used to say it. However, discourses are not fixed systems. On the contrary, discourses do get reworked and overturned but the mechanisms by which this occurs are not necessarily those which are argued in traditional analyses of history and culture, for example, cataclysmic events such as wars and revolutions (Macfarlane, 2006). For the postmodernist, then, discourses produce particular notions of truth and taken-for-granted understandings, which must be deconstructed in order to understand the effects of power.

Poststructuralism

Kinchloe and McLaren (2000) argue that postmodernism and poststructuralism should not be considered together. Postmodernists focus on language and discourse, as explained above. Poststructuralist researchers are interested in the analytical possibilities of language use and its relationship to truth and power. For poststructuralists, nothing exists outside discourse.

Postructuralism is a useful tool as it allows for the deconstruction of particular instances, practices or events, leading to more thorough analysis and the understanding that there is no neutral place from which to conduct research. For poststructuralists, our common-sense 'reality' is constituted in language or, more precisely, in patterns of language use (Macfarlane, 2006). 'Discourse' is the term used in poststructuralist work to name these systems of language use, which are, at the same time, systems of power relations (Macfarlane, 2006). Poststructuralist researchers adhere to the idea that there are multiple ways of learning and knowing (DEEWR, 2010).

Both postmodernism and poststructuralism have recently influenced the field of early childhood in the form of reconceptualist scholarship. Perspectives such as feminism, queer theory, poststructuralism and post-colonialism have 'led to reconceptualisations of the purposes for education and care as well as a re-examination of research and practice' (Grieshaber & Cannella, 2001, p. 11). Professionals working in early childhood settings who come from a poststructuralist perspective would be likely to consider multiple perspectives when planning for work with young children and their families. Early childhood teachers would plan experiences that acknowledge the different experiences and ways of learning that children bring to the context. These teachers would also use different strategies for planning and assessment and multiple ways to interpret data (DEEWR, 2010). In the postmodern tradition, these professionals would also be aware that childhood is a social construction and that the image of the child can both constrain and enable practice.

Foucauldian theory

Although there would be some contestation in some quarters about categorising Foucault as a poststructuralist, we believe that his theory is best dealt with in this section.

Truth

Foucault's original ideas relating to truth, power and governmentality (Foucault, 1978, 1979, 1980) significantly added to re-theorising social practice. According to Foucault (1980), the ways in which people understand what is 'true' and 'false' produces certain 'truth effects' – particular modes of address, vocabularies, activities, behaviours and so on (Macfarlane, 2006). Foucault is concerned with 'games of truth and error' (Foucault, 1985, p. 6), referring to the construction of 'truth' through discursive practices (1980). Foucault understands discourse as producing social and systemic practice by means of the constitution of 'regimes of truth' (1980, p. 131) that govern such practices. This includes expressions of the values of particular institutions engaged in these practices (Macfarlane, 2006). Foucault attests that:

> Each society has its regime of truth, its 'general politics' of truth; that is, the types of discourse which it accepts and makes function as true: the mechanisms and instances which enable one to distinguish true and false statements, the means by which each is sanctioned; the techniques and procedures accorded value in the acquisition of truth; the status of those who are charged with saying what counts as true. (1980, p. 131)

In Foucauldian terms, then, the researcher is analysing how certain 'regimes of truth' (1980, p. 131) work to objectify and subjectify individuals.

Power

According to Foucauldian theory, power is viewed as productive in both positive and negative ways. Foucault's theory can be seen to be quite different from the traditional conceptualisations of power, which do not sufficiently explain how particular events are possible (Macfarlane, 2006). As Foucault (1980) did not hold with the neo-Marxist principle of an all-powerful state, his analytic of power is useful in that it is posed in terms of how power is exercised rather than what it is, where it comes from or who holds it (Dreyfus & Rabinow, 1982; Hatcher, 1997). Foucault (1978, 1979, 1991) suggests that the shift from sovereign power to practices of discipline and government began as the need to discipline societies became greater (Macfarlane, 2006). As populations became larger, it became necessary to require that individuals become more and more obedient and techniques to control the population needed to be more finely tuned (Dreyfus & Rabinow, 1982; Hatcher, 1997).

Foucault (1978, 1979, 1980) deals with two distinct conceptions of power that characterise the modern period (Macfarlane, 2006). These are disciplinary power and bio-power, both distinct though overlapping and both producing particular forms of subjectification (Dreyfus & Rabinow, 1982; Hatcher, 1997; Meredyth & Tyler, 1993). Foucault's concept of disciplinary power is discussed as operating primarily on the body (Macfarlane, 2006). The aim of disciplinary technology is to create 'a "docile" [body] that may be subjected, used, transformed and improved' (Foucault, 1979, p. 136). According to Foucault, in order for disciplinary power to operate successfully, a certain standard of everyday behaviour needs to be made apparent (Macfarlane, 2006). This form of 'normalising judgement' (Dreyfus & Rabinow, 1982, p. 158), means that individuals need to conform to a certain type of behaviour or they can become the object of disciplinary attention (Macfarlane, 2006). The nonconformist, even the temporary one, becomes the object of attention and is singled out and disciplined in some way (Dreyfus & Rabinow, 1982). Individuals engaging in unruly behaviour are disciplined not only by those accorded with the status of deciding 'truth' about behaviour, but often by the general community as well (Macfarlane, 2006).

While disciplinary power deals mostly with the objectification of the individual in Foucault's earlier work, bio-power is concerned with the control of particular populations for the sake of increased productivity (Dreyfus & Rabinow, 1982; Foucault, 1978; Hatcher, 1997). What Foucault terms 'bio-power' is his interpretation of the relationship between sex, truth, power, the body and the individual (Macfarlane, 2006). According to Fraser, bio-power represents modern power, which is unlike earlier conceptualisations of power in that it is 'local, continuous, productive, capillary and exhaustive' (Fraser, 1989, p. 22). Bio-power has gained momentum with the increases in scientific and humanistic knowledge and the ability of those with this knowledge to examine and analyse the population (Dreyfus & Rabinow, 1982; Macfarlane, 2006). With the advance of this knowledge and examination comes the ability to categorise individuals, thereby creating and distinguishing, for instance, 'normal' from 'delinquent' or 'pervert'. This means that certain behaviours become normalised and others become abnormal (Macfarlane, 2006).

Governmentality

An important aspect of Foucault's conceptualisation of bio-power is his concept of the 'art of government' or 'governmentality' (Foucault, 1978, 1991). Foucault preferred to conceive of power as a strategy in which subjects are both productively engaged and normalised (Hatcher, 1997). The individual, then, already discursively produced, 'freely' chooses to act in ways consistent or inconsistent with the regimes of truth that exist at any given historical time (Macfarlane, 2006). As the state is comprised of practices of government, for example schools, businesses, and professional organisations, the particular regimes of truth that exist in these organisations in turn work to make a civil society (Rose, 1990, 1999) by governing individuals within them (Macfarlane, 2006). The subject is not forced to behave in a particular way, but rather self-regulates his/her activities in response to certain normalised practices. As certain behaviours are normalised by the regimes of truth that exist in society and as modern subjects come to understand these 'truths', they are more likely to self-regulate their behaviour and become more easily governed (Foucault, 1978, 1984b). The workings of power are less visible as certain behaviours are considered 'proper' (Macfarlane, 2006). Thus, Foucauldian researchers are concerned with documenting how certain truth effects are produced by discourse and consequently how such discourses work to govern certain behaviours and practices.

Genealogy

Genealogy is a research method that was used extensively by Foucault in the examination of social and systemic practice. Genealogy is an effective method to use because of its ability to enable the terms by which problems are currently understood to become objects of inquiry (Macfarlane, 2006). Termed 'history of the present' (Foucault, 1983, p. 118), genealogy seeks to 'emancipate historical knowledges' (Gordon, 1980, p. 85), allowing them a legitimate role in questioning the more formal and accepted scientific discourses which, through their familiarity, produce many of our social and systemic practices (Macfarlane, 2006).

Genealogy conceptualises anomalies as 'problems of the present' (Foucault, 1983, 1984a; Meredyth & Tyler, 1993; Tamboukou & Ball, 2003). The approach works in the tradition of deconstructive critique, as both a method and a task (Meadmore, Hatcher, & McWilliam, 2000). It is a departure from critical theory and critical ethnography in that the genealogist treats history not as a march of progress, but rather as a series of 'jolts', 'surprises', 'unsteady victories' and 'unpalatable defeats' (Foucault, 1984a, p. 80). While a Critical theoretical approach to the study would focus on the resistances within the event as an ideological struggle, a genealogical approach deals with the locality and plurality of resistances (Macfarlane, 2006). Genealogy uses a historical framework although not in a traditional sense. Rather than understanding history as a prolonged, linear-cumulative battle, this approach focuses on ways that minor and local events are connected or disconnected to produce other events, truths and practices (Macfarlane, 2006). Consequently, genealogy refuses the hierarchical ranking of knowledge and the linearity of traditional historical approaches, allowing space to be created for discontinuities, accidents and disqualified knowledges that are vital to the production of an event (Foucault, 1984a; Gordon, 1980; Grieshaber & Cannella, 2001; Hatcher, 1997; Meadmore et al., 2000).

Understood in this way, genealogy works as an 'interpretive analytic' (Dreyfus & Rabinow, 1982, p. 122) to reveal the contingency of human history, while not attempting to uncover hidden meanings of the type sought in neo-Marxist ideology critique (Hatcher, 1997; Tyler & Johnson, 1991). Genealogy does not seek to understand what might be behind certain historical events or behaviours, but elaborates on 'the surfaces of events, small details, minor shifts and subtle contours' (Dreyfus & Rabinow, 1982, p. 106) as being productive of a particular event.

For Foucault, the examination of a particular incident at the local level makes it possible to take into account the understandings of those directly involved in the particular struggle, to value their knowledge and their understanding of how the event was possible. By opening up the multiple ways knowledge is produced, genealogy gives a more complete understanding of the conditions of possibility that produce an event. Thus, genealogy attempts to conceptualise problems of the present in alternative ways from how traditional or revisionist histories have understood and described them (Macfarlane, 2006).

Applying theoretical perspectives

Each theoretical perspective mentioned above clearly has its own characteristics and its 'rules' of use. However, here is how Lara approached her research project:

> I approached my research with three sections in my mind, philosophy, strategy and methodology. I knew that I was going to conduct qualitative research so I learned that that implied an inductive, theory-generating approach. I then studied the various qualitative perspectives and settled upon phenomenology. I did get bogged down in the origins of this movement and my biggest piece of advice would be something I was told at the time: you are not writing a thesis on phenomenology. You do need to know about it, of course, but you do not need to be the world expert. You just need to be able to competently use and apply the approach, and explain this in writing and verbally to others.

Lara's advice is useful in helping researchers to think realistically about what they can hope to achieve within the boundaries of time available when they are working on a project. She highlights the complexity of the journey and suggests that research is an ongoing rather than a limited journey.

To further illustrate some of the complexities involved in applying particular theoretical perspectives and aligning methodologies to answer certain research questions, we turn to Sarah's research journey.

Sarah was a three-year trained early childhood teacher who returned to study in 1996. Following the completion of her fourth year, Sarah decided to enter the doctoral studies program so that she could complete this qualification and move to the university sector. As an early childhood teacher trained in the 1970s, Sarah had a very romantic view of childhood and her work with young children and their families. She had a very strong image of the child as an explorer who learned through play. She also believed that the teacher should act as a facilitator and largely not interfere in young children's play. Additionally, growing up in a working-class family had led to Sarah developing strong views of life that could be considered 'left of centre'. Sarah's way of viewing the world aligned with Critical theory. She had a strong ideological understanding that adhered to the notion that the state would always hold the ultimate power and a belief in emancipatory rhetoric. However, when she decided to begin her doctorate, she chose to use poststructuralist theory as her theoretical framework, most particularly, the work of Michel Foucault. This choice presented Sarah with some challenges. First, poststructuralist writing has a certain tone that is quite different from the tone used in Critical theory. The tone in poststructuralist writing can be ironic and will highlight inconsistencies. Poststructuralist writers develop arguments but not in terms of pointing out rights and wrongs, but rather in highlighting the problematic. This method of writing aligns with their idea of using or considering multiple perspectives and also with the notion that there is no absolute or universal truth.

Sarah's choice became a difficult one. When writing, she wanted to draw conclusions and apportion blame, which was highly problematic when using the poststructuralist style of writing. Sarah constantly had to challenge her natural way of writing to ensure she was remaining as true to her theoretical framework as possible (given that it was poststructural and therefore not claiming one true way). Sometimes her writing needed to be so particular that she almost had to decide word for word. This issue with writing, although ongoing to some extent, was eventually overcome. However, that was not the end of Sarah's issues.

Sarah had chosen to use genealogy as her methodological framework. Genealogy requires a painstaking analysis of text in rhetoric, documents and policy. Such analysis is almost undoable in that it can seem never-ending. As Sarah progressed, she developed a knowledge object at one point in the process that she wanted to investigate further. This knowledge object was an idea that Sarah developed that had not been identified or examined by anyone else. The fact that Sarah wanted to pursue the theorising related to this knowledge object meant that her writing and method became less genealogical. Thus, she had to decide how to proceed.

In consultation with her supervisors, Sarah decided to use *bricolage* (Lévi-Strauss, 1966) (see Chapter 8 which provides an in-depth coverage of *bricolage*) as her umbrella approach to her work. The use of *bricolage* allowed her to still use aspects of poststructuralism, but to craft these aspects in ways that allowed her investigation of her knowledge object to continue. Her work eventually included the overarching methodology of *bricolage*, a case study analysed using a genealogical approach and a re-theorising that included an examination of her newly developed knowledge objects. She was careful to use the work of Foucault as her main theorist and researchers who had applied Foucault's work in order to maintain epistemological coherence.

Sarah's discomfit with her work continued to some extent to its end. She was concerned that she had not stayed with the original choice of genealogy as method. She constantly struggled with the idea that while poststructuralist writing was difficult, it definitely suited her research questions. She did not want to move away from this theoretical framework but she did want to highlight the complexity of her research. Sarah was not yet aware of the fact that research is a messy and disparate process that does not always follow a seamless path. When she was able to understand this idea, she became more relaxed with her choices.

Sarah's journey is indicative of many journeys along the research path. She met with many obstacles but, by staying true to her research approaches, she was able to produce a strong thesis, which was very well received. Sarah's story is representative of the fact that research can be difficult and painstaking but, when the journey is complete, it can also prove rewarding and is always a learning experience.

HOW ARE SOME OF THESE APPROACHES CHANGING THE EARLY CHILDHOOD RESEARCH LANDSCAPE?

Some of the aforementioned research approaches are changing the early childhood landscape. First, postcolonial and poststructuralist theories are challenging the image of the child that early childhood professionals might hold. This sector, largely governed by Piagetian theory (Piaget, 1951) from the 1970s, has had an image of the child driven by romantic understandings in many respects. From the 1970s, the practice of many staff in early childhood education and care settings was underpinned by developmentally appropriate practice and by a culture of non-interference in children's play. These notions have now been challenged to include many images of childhood as a result of poststructuralist theory and an understanding informed by postcolonial theory, that our notions of children's development were ethnocentric. The focus on Foucauldian theory that came to prominence in the 1990s has added to these new understandings of childhood and development and has driven the reconceptualist movement in early childhood. Reconceptualists challenge taken-for-granted understandings of practice and notions of childhood, seeking to see practice being more informed by multiple perspectives rather than regimes of truth (Foucault, 1980). Early childhood researchers in the UK have also been informed by Foucauldian theory, bringing to prominence new work around the social construction of childhood.

Feminist theory has impacted on the early childhood sector since the late 1980s with new understandings of the influence of gender and oppression affecting practice in relation to how children's play is organised and designed. Similarly, hermeneutical inquiry and narrative inquiry have challenged our understandings of interpretation, leading to questions around observation of children and the participation of children in research. All of these approaches have had some impact and have changed the way in which early childhood research has been undertaken.

An example of such a change is seen in the work of Deborah Tyler in the 1990s. Tyler uses a genealogical analysis of child development literature to demonstrate how a certain type of citizen can be produced, and examines the mechanisms used to work towards such an outcome (Macfarlane, 2006). She argues that child development literature has, over time, promoted the virtues of the preschool as a mechanism for directing children towards rationality, autonomy and self-regulation. This assisted in enabling a teacher to direct the child towards social desirability. Tyler (1993, p. 44) states:

> Alongside rationality, the better child would move steadily toward total independence by taking every opportunity to exercise greater control and autonomy. For the child to be moving towards independence, also meant taking responsibility for one's self and one's actions, and discovering that the desire to do something was not sufficient reason for doing it. But the child who was forced into obedience would never discover 'inner discipline' and would come only to resent the rules, and not regulate the self. The child was capable of self-regulation, and to realise its full potential must develop this capacity.

Tyler's argument is that the architecture and organisation of space in the preschool worked in certain ways to increase surveillance of children and maintain the capacity for self-regulation. She proposes that certain non-coercive techniques were used to achieve this and that these became part of the practices within these preschool organisations.

The surveillance, normalisation and individualisation of young children are still very much a part of early childhood educational philosophy (Grieshaber & Cannella, 2001; Jenks, 1996) and are an example of how non-coercive techniques can be used to create a certain type of citizen (Rose, 1999, 2000). According to Paul Hirst (1986), surveillance is '…crucial to the transformation of subjects into beings of a particular type, whose conduct is patterned and governed and who are endowed with definite attributes and abilities' (in Tyler, 1993, p. 46).

It can be seen in Tyler's research how using certain theoretical perspectives might transform what we believe to be true about our work in early childhood. Tyler's work creates a different picture, which encourages us to challenge our taken-for-granted assumptions about children, childhood and observation. Such work can enrich our understanding and our practices as it assists us to see our regimes of truth in a new light.

WHAT DOES THIS MEAN FOR EARLY CHILDHOOD PRACTICE?

Venturing into these perspectives has meant that richer research in early childhood is possible. For example, questioning taken-for-granted understandings has meant that early childhood researchers have been able to illuminate new understandings about practice. The focus on Piaget (1951) has been lessened with other understandings, such as those of Vygotsky (1978), Bronfenbrenner (1979), Rogoff (2003) and Malaguzzi (1993), coming to the fore. The work of Foucault has enabled marginalised understandings of children, childhood and families to be made visible. This has meant that practice in early childhood has become more varied and has been opened up to new ways of thinking. Our image of the child has been challenged and, in many cases, has been replaced by multiple understandings of children, childhood and families, which has prompted discussion. This process has minimised possibilities for marginalisation. There is also now more of a focus on the voices of children and the professional's relationship with children and families. This relationship is now one of collegiality, collaboration and co-construction, and not one of expert and student. This means that there are many opportunities for research to be undertaken in ways that allow this co-construction to occur.

REFLECTION POINTS

When considering which theoretical perspective you will choose for your research, use the following questions to guide you:

- Which approach best reflects my epistemological and ontological stance as a researcher?
- Which approach would best fit with my research topic or question(s)?
- Which research approaches 'speak' to me when I think about my research?
- What am I concerned most with – people and relationships or are my questions more pragmatic?
- What image of the child do I hold and how might that impact on the approach I take to my research?
- Is this image limiting my options?

☐ **Summary**

In this chapter we have examined a range of different perspectives that are being applied to research in early childhood. Some of these may be familiar to you but others may be new. This chapter has provided a taste of these approaches so that you may consider whether to include them as part of your research journey. The chapter has:

- outlined a number of theoretical perspectives that guide research;
- highlighted the impact of these theoretical perspectives on research and practice in early childhood.

BEGINNING THE RESEARCH JOURNEY: DETERMINING YOUR POINT OF DEPARTURE

This chapter outlines what is required when beginning a research project. It provides guidance on selecting a topic for the study, determining the aims of the research, framing research questions and developing a research proposal. To help make the practical application of the information more understandable, we present the thinking of Amy and Lara about their research journeys. This gives an insight into the process of topic selection and the beginning stages of the research journey they each experienced.

Key chapter questions are:

- Where do I start?
- How do I select a topic?
- How do I define the aim(s) of the research?
- How do I frame research questions?
- What is the purpose of a research proposal and how do I develop one?
- What else needs considering?

WHERE DO I START?

The first thing that you need to realise is that there is a process to follow when undertaking a research project. The usual process follows the sequence of selecting a topic, reviewing the literature related to the topic, defining the aims or focus of the research, which gives rise to the research question or questions, and then designing the research project (considering methodology and methods). The chapter has been organised according to this sequence, concluding with a section of other aspects that need consideration.

HOW DO I SELECT A TOPIC?

Take time when selecting your topic. When looking for an issue to investigate or a problem to solve, Burns (2000) suggests that there are three important sources to consider, these being related literature, theory (the testing of theories leading to theory generation) and experience. Topics could include examining aspects relating to the health, welfare, education or care of young children, or a combination of these. As most research involves a time investment, it is always a good idea, where possible, to choose an area of interest. It will help sustain you throughout the project, especially during times when you begin questioning why you began the project in the first place. Reading literature related to an area of interest is a good way to begin to understand the area, the status of current research in that area and to identify research issues that you may want to investigate further.

When you start thinking about your personal experience, you may be surprised how many topics come to mind. Try considering the issues, events or actions that have you reflecting and sharing with others. Consider if one of these could be utilised as a starter topic to explore further. For example, many early childhood teachers and practitioners use the issues that they face on a daily basis as a starting point for further investigation, such as how young children prepare for or transition into school environments, the impact of effective learning environments on children's learning, or reflections on their own practice, such as how literacy is embedded within their program or how children respond to their questioning techniques.

Amy, one of two researchers whose research journeys we are following throughout this book, discusses her interest in her topic, which came from her personal experience of being a mother.

> The title of my research was: 'Relationships between infant toddler pretend play, maternal interactions and later child IQ: a longitudinal study'. I was really exploring early gifted development and I did that by looking at the pretend play development of a group of infants and toddlers and that was taken as a measure of their cognitive development and the maternal interactions in that development and how they promoted children's play and thinking, certain forms of thinking, and I then assessed the children on an IQ measure when they turned 5 years of age.

> One of my sons had been assessed as he was having trouble learning to read and he'd been assessed as gifted when he was 5 and he'd just started school. He was having a lot of trouble learning to read, which I probably picked up because I was an early childhood teacher. Somebody else probably wouldn't even have noticed. He was assessed as having mild dyslexia but also as being

gifted so I got quite interested in gifted development. I also had a friend, a mother of a child in my son's class, and he had a younger sister who was about 2 years of age at the time and she was an interesting child. She actually had a mild hemiplegia, but she was so intelligent and so socially aware. The maturity of her mind was extraordinary. Her mother said 'Yes she's very bright' and that hemiplegia is often associated with high IQ, however her son was bright as well. He'd been diagnosed as gifted. I looked at the interaction that occurred between this mother and daughter and it started the idea crossing my mind 'Do parents of children with higher IQ interact with them differently from other parents?' So that was the beginning of it.

I was interested because it raises issues about the nature of giftedness with the genetics and the environmental influences. But not just giftedness, it's the whole thing of intellectual development. I don't have fixed ideas about what giftedness is. I see IQ as just one of many indicators of what can be advanced thinking or development. So it's just the whole issue I suppose, of early intellectual development and what promotes it. I think gifted development is an interesting sort of example of intellectual development that can perhaps teach us things about intellectual development across the whole population.

As Amy's journey demonstrates, the research must focus on one specific aspect of a topic otherwise it is too broad and wide in scope. This is an ongoing process where you continue to refine your thinking about the topic. In other words, it has to be 'do-able' in time, interest, resources, and complexity. The following steps may assist you in the process:

- Note your ideas or areas of interest;
- Think about what each one might be asking you to do as a researcher;
- Brainstorm all the possibilities and thoughts you have in relation to this topic area;
- Use this information to reflect further, clarifying your thoughts and becoming clearer on what your research could be aiming to achieve.

Do not be surprised if you need to repeat this process a number of times to clarify your thoughts and find a way forward.

Find some colleagues, fellow students and critical friends with whom to discuss your initial thoughts. As Bell (2010) suggests, friends and colleagues 'may be aware of sensitive aspects of certain topics which could cause difficulties at some stages or they may know of other people who have carried out research in one or more of your topics who would be willing to talk to you' (p. 29). Read some of the already completed research that has been conducted in the area and discuss this with others. The more times you have to explain your interest and possible research topic the more it will become refined from the questions, comments and feedback of your listeners. Once you are at this point you are ready to consider the aim or purpose of the study.

For some projects the topic may already be set, especially if the research project is commissioned by an internal body or external organisation. In this case the researcher may be able to influence the research question(s), shaping them to fit, as much as possible, with the researcher's own interests or agenda while still fulfilling the outcomes as set down by the funding body. For example, a researcher may be interested in reflective practice, a topic which could become a sub-theme in a larger study. By working in this way, your project may be able to add capacity to the findings of the overall study.

A conversation with Lara, the other researcher we are following, outlines her initial thoughts about topic areas and how her research project (supported by a studentship) needed to be carefully considered so that it met the criteria and expectations of the scholarship.

> I undertook doctoral research. It was entitled 'An investigation exploring the experiences of a range of practitioners using graphic symbols with children in Foundation Stage (3–5 years) school settings'. My research started as a project that was going to include two key topics. One was the way that graphic symbols were used with young children and the other was professional collaboration in a Foundation Stage setting with children aged 3–5 years. I took those two topics and decided to really bring them together, so I looked at using graphic symbols with that age group as a way to do this. I chose this as there is more than one professional group involved and I wanted to know how the professionals involved collaborated, if indeed they were collaborating. Through looking at the literature, I identified teachers, early years practitioners (EYPs) (teaching assistants, learning support assistants and nursery nurses), and speech and language therapists (SLTs) as the three groups most likely to be involved.

> I had been working as a teaching assistant in schools with the age group in the UK and using Makaton signs and symbols (Makaton is a communication technique using signs and symbols to aid children experiencing learning difficulties). I was looking to change jobs and I identified a studentship which was a doctoral project that was going to be located near where I was living, and it was, basically, perfect timing. So I was lucky enough to be chosen for it.

> I'd say my interest changed over time because when I started it was the symbols that attracted me to the project, but by the end of it the major outcome of the project was much more a framework looking at collaborative practice, with the use of symbols as an applied example of that, or a context in which that would apply.

When asked about whether she felt any pressure that her research had to be conducted in a certain way, Lara responded as follows:

> I did, but I just relaxed about this over time. I remember my supervisor saying that is all right. There were only very few times when I would say something

and they would say 'Well, this is funded by speech language therapy so we need to keep you here', but this happened only a very few times. It was my decision for it to cover mainstream and special education; it was my decision for it to have quite a strong psychology theme; it was my decision for it to be just the Foundation Stage.

HOW DO I DEFINE THE AIM(S) OF THE RESEARCH?

Once you define your topic, then you must next decide on the actual aims of the research study you will undertake. By clarifying the overarching aims you are able to generate research questions that meet these aims (Mukherji & Albon, 2010). Ask yourself what you are hoping to achieve by undertaking the study to determine the aims and objectives.

To assist with refining your research aims (leading into the framing of your research question(s)), Burton and Bartlett (2005) offer the following prompts:

- Why research this area?
- What precisely is it that you want to find out about?
- Is there a desire to change anything? If so, what and why?

Reflecting on the topic and aim or purpose will assist in defining 'researchable questions' (Laws, with Harper, & Marcus, 2003, p. 97) so use this information to inform the next stage of the process – framing the research question(s). Again, this will help you clarify what it is you are trying to achieve by undertaking the research project, which in turn will impact on the type of approach you take (see Chapters 7 and 8 for a detailed explanation of these approaches).

Hatch (2007) reminds us that to rush into research without undertaking a careful consideration of theoretical perspectives can lead to a research project that is ill-conceived and illogical. Consideration needs to be given to the theoretical perspectives within which the study will be located which will add clarity to the research aims (see Chapter 3). Ontological assumptions, along with epistemological assumptions, need to be identified to enable the research to be located within a suitable theoretical perspective. This also ensures that 'decisions about research approaches are logically consistent' (Hatch, 2007, p. 226). Once a research approach within a theoretical perspective is chosen, the research question(s) can then be located within this framework. Taking time to clarify these issues will see a better fit between aims, research question(s) and basic assumptions. 'The questions selected should build logically from the researcher's theoretical orientation and substantive interests' (Hatch, 2007, p. 232).

HOW DO I FRAME RESEARCH QUESTIONS?

Once the limits of the study have been defined, empirical issues identified, and the research study itself clarified, it is time to 'work on empirical questions' (Clough & Nutbrown, 2007, p. 37). Selecting the research questions is one of the most crucial decisions that someone embarking on a research project has to make as they impact on the research design, providing a consistent thread through the components of the design (Maxwell, 1996). This is not as easy a process as it may at first appear, but it is one that needs to align with the aims of the study which have already been determined. The questions provide a point of reference throughout the study, although the questions may change or be modified during a study. For example, a common problem is that the project is scoped too widely, trying to 'save the world' instead of identifying a more defined, specific question or hypothesis to test that will address the aims and focus of the research project. To keep a check on the research process itself, researchers can ask themselves whether the data they are collecting or the way the data is being processed is answering the question(s) and meeting the original intention of the research.

It is common for most research projects to begin with one overarching question, under which other, interrelated questions can sit. By working through the interrelated questions, the main question is answered. The main question should signal the intent of the project and the scope (the boundaries and breadth). Hatch (2007) suggests that the questions for qualitative studies need to be 'open-ended, few in number, and stated in a straightforward language' (p. 231), whereas more closed questions are better addressed by quantitative studies. The questions have to be able to be answered through some type of data collection and analysis, and here lies another problem that faces researchers – being specific enough to know exactly what information to focus on that will address the identified aims.

For research taking a more qualitative approach, a way to work through this process is to develop what you think is your main question and then brainstorm all the sub-questions that could be related to this main question. Take time to think carefully about each of these questions and exactly what each is asking. You may find it helpful to write a statement qualifying each question so that the intention of the question is clear. Once you have done this you may begin to see synergies between some of the questions and these can then be grouped together. By grouping similar questions together you will be able to judge whether or not the similar questions are asking for the same information. This will help you eliminate duplication and assist in aligning the questions to the research aims. The questions also need to be ordered so that there is a logical flow, with each question complementing the others while building towards answering the original question and addressing the study's aims. This is a time-consuming process and can cause frustration. It takes time to reflect on all the possible questions, considering the direction in which each can take the research. However, it is an essential part of the process, ensuring that you have a well-considered research project.

One novice researcher, Janine, taking a qualitative approach, wanted to investigate mentoring relationships within an experiential learning program for pre-service early childhood teachers. The program involved pre-service early childhood teachers working with mentors, university colleagues and communities in 25 sites across two regions of a major capital city in the development, implementation and evaluation of supported community playgroups for children under school age in collaboration with their parents or guardians. She set her initial question as 'What is the role of the mentor in the program?' The program featured a formal mentoring role for a designated person. However, on further reflection, it became apparent that perhaps informal mentoring was also occurring between the student teachers themselves. Janine was then faced with the challenge of widening the scope of the original research question to look at the nature of mentoring within the program. The change meant a re-focusing of the research to incorporate a wider construction of mentoring within the program. More exploratory questions about informal mentoring relationships were added to the original research question.

WHAT IS THE PURPOSE OF A RESEARCH PROPOSAL AND HOW DO I DEVELOP ONE?

There is often a need to develop a research proposal that outlines the design of the project so that it can be presented to others, such as a research committee or ethics committee, for approval. A research proposal should be a well-thought-through document which clearly articulates the what, when, where, who, why, and how of the proposed research project.

What is this research project going to be about?

What is the research question or hypothesis?

Why is this research project important and to whom is it important?

When is the research to take place?

Where will the research take place?

How will the research project be conducted?

Who are the subjects or participants of the research?

There are particular expectations and processes around writing a research proposal.

A research proposal usually takes the following form:

- Introduction and overview, including the aims, background and research question(s) or hypothesis;
- Literature review (summary);
- Methodology or conceptual orientation;
- Methods of data collection and data analysis to be employed; and
- Project management details, such as a Gantt chart which will illustrate the timeline for the project.

Developing a research proposal

To help understand exactly what a proposal could look like (remembering this does vary depending on your institution's or organisation's guidelines and the purpose of the proposal), excerpts from a successful research proposal have been incorporated throughout this section of the chapter. This proposal is written by Elizabeth Rouse, who was a doctoral student. The title of Elizabeth's research was 'Effective family partnerships in early childhood education and care – an investigation of the nature of interactions between educators and parents'. Her research question, at the time of the proposal, was 'How effective is the nature of the interactions between parents and early childhood practitioners in developing genuine partnerships between the educators and the parents, as determined by a partnership framework of mutuality, trust and reciprocity?' In order to present a proposal to the university where she undertook her studies, two senior academics had to read and provide feedback on the proposal. One of the reviewers was so impressed that she requested permission to use Elizabeth's research proposal as an example to show other students. For this reason, we think it is important to incorporate her work into this chapter.

Any research proposal needs to be written in a clear and accessible style, taking into consideration the audience of the document. The introduction and overview section of the proposal should provide a clear outline of the research to be undertaken, defining the topic, aim or purpose of the study and the research question or hypothesis to be proven or disproven. A clear statement of the contribution to existing knowledge that the research will make, what needs are satisfied by this research, along with an explanation of the significance of the study, is also included. In some cases it may be necessary to define key terms if these are not self-explanatory in the proposal itself.

The following excerpts from Elizabeth's proposal for candidature (a process that student researchers have to go through in some institutions in some countries in order to have their enrolment into a higher degree course confirmed) show how a study can be framed.

Introduction

The early childhood education and care sector in Australia is being recognised for the important role it plays in determining the long-term benefits and outcomes for children. A key focus of the current Government is for Australian children to 'have access to high-quality early learning and care' and this government has placed early childhood education and care at the forefront of the national agenda of the Council of Australian Governments (COAG).

A national Early Years Learning Framework has been developed as a response to the Council of Australian Governments' (COAG) concern to address the quality of early childhood education and care across Australia. This framework places a heavy emphasis on quality learning and development programs for educators in achieving best outcomes for children. A key determinant of a quality learning program, as presented within this framework, is the relationship that educators develop with parents and families as equal partners in the education and care of young children. The framework recognises that 'learning outcomes are most likely to be achieved when early childhood educators work in partnership with families' (p. 12).

In Victoria, the state government has recently released the Victorian Early Years Learning and Development Framework (0–8), referred to as the Victorian Framework, that describes common goals for children from birth to age eight across all early childhood education and care programs, and linking into the first three years of schooling. The development of this framework was undertaken concurrent to the national framework, and was informed by the national framework, to provide a local focus for early years educators in Victoria. A key principle in this framework is a strong acknowledgement of the role of parents as the first and most enduring educators of children and a focus for educators on constructive partnerships with parents within a framework of family-centred practice (pp. 9–10).

As can be seen in this excerpt from Elizabeth's introduction of her pro-posal, she has provided a clear picture of the early childhood scene and how her topic is a focus of current policy initiatives. She begins with a national view and then continues to refine this by outlining the view held at a state level, in this case the state of Victoria in Australia. The reader is thus aware of the importance being placed on this aspect of teachers' work at a national level and how this has translated to the state where the research will be conducted. This background informa-tion provides a platform for her to then build the rationale for the study.

Research proposals need to state the aim(s) of the project clearly, along with the contribution to knowledge it will make and the significance of the research study to the field.

Aim

The aim of this research is to investigate the nature of the interactions between parents and educators to provide an understanding of the extent to which these interactions may be defined as family-centred practice. The research aims to reflect on these interactions as occurring within a model of partnership, as determined by a theoretical construct of partnership as mutuality, trust and reciprocity (Dunst & Dempsey, 2007; Kruger, Davies, Eckersley, Newell, & Cherednichenko, 2009).

As can be seen with the aim(s) section of this candidate's proposal, there is a flow from the background and larger policy context down to the specific purpose of this study. There is an understandable focus with obvious links to the current policy context, as outlined in the background section of the proposal, and a direct link to the research question.

Elizabeth provides a strong rationale for her study and then builds on this by presenting the related literature.

Rationale

While policy and learning frameworks espouse the importance of early childhood educators engaging in genuine partnerships with parents and families, there is little research that provides evidence of current practice and outcomes, and even less that provides a local and contemporary focus. There have been only a small number of studies undertaken in Australia over the past decade that examine the nature of the engagement of parents in the education and care of their children in early childhood programs.

...While there is a wealth of literature examining and evaluating family-centred practice as it relates to early intervention programs, highlighting its strengths and positive outcomes for families (Johnson, 2000; Keen, 2007; Raghavendra, Murchland, Bentley, Wake-Dyster, & Lyons, 2007), little if any research that examines this model as creating effective partnerships with families of young children who do not have additional development or medical needs has been conducted.

In the following paragraph we see how the candidate continues to build her justification as to the importance of the proposed research.

The Victorian State Government has recognised that there is a need to investigate 'models of partnerships with early childhood service providers, parents and communities that are the most effective in achieving strong learning and developmental outcomes' (Department of Education and Early Childhood Development, *Research Priority Areas of Interest 2008–2011*, 2008, p. 4). Within this context, it is important to understand the model of family-centred practice and to examine this model as it defines the nature of the interactions between parents and early childhood educators in early childhood education and care programs in Victoria. While there is a strong emphasis on the importance of developing partnerships with parents, because of the paucity of contemporary literature examining models of partnership, there is a need to better understand the nature of the interactions that currently exist between educators and parents across the early childhood sector and the extent to which these can be defined as family-centred practice.

In Elizabeth's examination of this question, the following more specific questions were also used to inform the data collection and analysis:

- To what extent can the nature of the interactions between parents and early childhood educators be defined as family-centred practice?
- To what extent is the nature of the interactions between parents and early childhood educators influenced by the socio-cultural experiences of the participants?

Contributions to knowledge, along with the significance of the study, also need to be included in a research proposal and have been represented in Elizabeth's proposal as follows:

Contribution to knowledge

This study will build a body of knowledge that provides an understanding of the nature of interactions between educators and parents in early childhood education and care programs and an insight into how the socio-cultural experiences of the participants may influence the relationship. This understanding will generate a deeper knowledge of how family-centred practice, as a model of partnership, is played out in early childhood education and care settings.

Significance to the field

In response to a lack of clarity and guidelines to support educators in the implementation of family-centred practice as a model of partnership, the research will be of significance to the field in that it will provide an informed framework that will lead to the development of guidelines for professional practice for early childhood educators to support them in the engagement of effective partnerships with families.

What follows next is a short literature review. This section of a research proposal comprises a brief review and analysis of the literature related to the proposed study – that is, the issues and conclusions reached by relevant authors. Its purpose is to establish the theoretical framework and background literature for the research project and should include the key literature on the topic, identifying any gaps in the literature, while also describing the link between your research project and the literature. These gaps also act to justify your choice of research question. This is your chance to demonstrate your awareness of the key theories and research in this area and how your research project relates to, extends or contests the current literature and research.

You will need to include a section where you detail the research project design and justify the intended methodology for collecting and analysing the data. Here you are providing justification of the approach taken to research the question(s) and hypothesis. Each method should be outlined, explaining the appropriateness of the chosen method to answer the research question(s) and be true to the aims. Details relating to who is to be involved and why they were chosen need to be included, along with a statement relating to the validity of the sample size. The method of analysis will also need to be justified. The following questions may help to guide the process:

- What is to be collected (data)?
- How will the data be collected?
- Why is this data and approach appropriate?
- From whom will the data be collected?
- What will need to be considered in the data collection?
- How will the data be analysed?

At this stage of the process it is usually sufficient to state the method without including the actual tool(s). For example, if you are going to administer a survey, then you do not need to include the survey questions unless they add clarity to your overall proposal.

It is usually expected that a research proposal will also include details relating to the timing of the project – that is, a timeline of when aspects of the process will be undertaken. Costings related to the conduct of the project could be requested, so you will need to check this with your own institution or organisation to see what support is available for undertaking research projects. A note relating to whether or not ethical approval through a committee or organisation is required in order for the research to commence may also be required in this section. Sometimes you may be asked to submit a budget if funding is available.

Oral defence or presentation

Some universities require their higher degree students to undertake a formal oral defence to confirm their candidature. This can take the form of presenting your research proposal to a panel of researchers and academics. While this can sound daunting, it does provide an opportunity to gain further feedback on your research proposal and often can alert you to ways to strengthen and enhance the project. Although the process is unique to each institution, it is similar in that the candidate submits the written proposal which is distributed to the panel members before the oral presentation date. Often, it is a requirement that one panel member is external to the university or organisation and brings expert knowledge related to the topic. It may be possible to use some type of visual presentation on the day to accompany the oral presentation, but this will need to be checked with individual institutions. It is important to remember that when you present your proposal, the panel members have read your complete proposal and so don't want to hear a lengthy re-hash of this. Instead, think of ways to expand on your written proposal, perhaps using illustrations (if allowed) or adding more context around the decisions you have made and why they are important to the design of your project. Try to be succinct and practise what you are going to say, because within a university environment the oral presentation may be open to the general university population and advertised widely, so there may be an audience other than the panel members themselves.

WHAT ELSE NEEDS CONSIDERING?

While you are working through these early stages of your research project, you will also need to begin considering the sensitivities regarding ethics and access that may surround your study. Topics involving more vulnerable groups, such as drug-addicted parents, children with atypical development, or teenage mothers can prove problematic and may not gain ethical approval from ethics committees if not well thought through. Sophie, a social worker undertaking a Masters program, chose the topic of parenting children with congenital heart defects. As the facilitator of a social networking site dedicated to supporting parents with children with this condition and as a parent of a 3-year-old diagnosed with a heart defect, the ethics committee cautioned her about the emotional sensitivities surrounding a topic that was so closely related to her personal circumstances. It was felt that she would not be able to distance herself in collecting and analysing her data and, as such, she was required to reshape her project to account for this potential conflict of interest. This was unanticipated and resulted in the rethinking of the research design.

Having considered the topic and aim(s) of the research, consideration can also be given to the selection of the research site – where the proposed research can be conducted. Attention needs to be directed to site selection early on to ensure that the researcher can access the site and that the participants at the site will have some interest in participating. Although in some sites initial access may be readily granted from the leader or administrator, the researcher may also have to negotiate access at other levels, for example at the classroom, or room level. This takes time and can be a complex process. In one study which focused on the exploration of an innovative preschool implementation model, access had to be negotiated at both the state and local government levels, followed by the individual preschool management committee level before the teachers and parents were asked about their interest in participating in the project. The lesson here is that prior to you going too far into your research planning you need to investigate possible sites and the level of access that is required, noting the process that you would need to undertake in order to gain this access. This may make you reconsider the intended site, which may also impact on the aims, research question(s) and design. You also need to be mindful that the research agenda in early childhood contexts can be quite broad, including other professionals and parents. For example, a project focusing on early childhood workforce development can encompass the perspectives of parents, teachers, practitioners, key stakeholders as well as children.

When your research intent is to involve young children, access can become even more problematic as ethical considerations (see discussion in Chapter 6) and gatekeepers will influence accessibility. If you follow this path, you may find that gatekeepers such as parents, teachers, social workers and allied health professionals can allow or disallow access to potential participants. Access can be hindered due to the sensitivity of the topic or research question, the perceived interest or capability of the children and the possible disruption caused by participation in the research (Dockett & Perry, 2011). Be prepared to negotiate access and strongly state the importance of having the child represented in the research project. You will also need to allow time for negotiations such as this to take place.

As outlined in this chapter, there is much to consider when beginning a research journey. For instance, researching with young children adds a complexity to the research design that must be considered at this early stage, such as framing the research from a rights perspective. As Kellett (2010, p. 81) suggests:

> The importance of constructing research involving children from a rights perspective cannot be underestimated. It foregrounds children's rights as human rights and challenges the legitimacy of research inquiry which does not take these rights into account. It emphasises the centrality and agency of children throughout the research process irrespective of whether the research is about, with or by children.

REFLECTION POINTS

In relation to beginning your own research work, use the following questions to guide your thinking:

- What topic am I considering?
- Why does this interest me?
- What has influenced my decisions to date?
- What is already known about this topic?
- Have I considered the 'pragmatic assumptions' (ontological assumptions and epistemological assumptions)? For example, what beliefs do I hold in relation to this topic?
- What do I consider are the main issues in relation to my proposed research?
- What did others have to say about my ideas?
- Have I defined clear aims for the study?
- How does my research question signal the intent and scope of the research project?

- Is there a logical flow from my theoretical orientation and interest to the aims and, subsequently, the research question or hypothesis?
- Is there a consistent thread throughout the project design?
- Have I considered the 'sensitive issues' that surround my project, especially if it involves young children?

☐   **Summary**

This chapter has focused on what needs to be considered when beginning your research project. Attention has focused on:

- taking time to develop a logical and well-conceived research project building from the researcher's theoretical orientation and substantive interests, through to the aims, research questions and approach; and
- presenting a well-thought-through research proposal.

5

KNOWING WHAT HAS GONE BEFORE: REVIEWING THE LITERATURE

This chapter focuses on how to conduct an effective literature review. It provides information on how to locate relevant literature, including assessing the strength of this literature, and how to summarise and critique it. Also outlined is how to present a report of the literature, incorporating how to synthesise and analyse information. Examples of how Amy and Lara approached their literature reviews are included so you can see how two novice researchers approached this task.

Key chapter questions are:

- What is the purpose of a literature review?
- What does a literature review involve?
- Where does a review of research methods fit?
- How do I identify literature related to my topic?
- How do I manage the material and when do I conclude a review?
- How do I evaluate and critique the research literature?
- How do I present a review?

WHAT IS THE PURPOSE OF A LITERATURE REVIEW?

A literature review shapes the research project, which should be informed by the gaps, omissions or unanswered questions found within previous research on a chosen topic – what has not been researched on the topic or what could be further investigated. This helps to formulate the aims and focus of the study which leads to the development of the research question(s) or hypothesis. It summarises the literature related to a particular field or event and it provides a background context for the research project. The literature review assists the researcher to situate

their own research project through understanding and critically reviewing previous research conducted in the area. It explores what has been
published on the topic and usually involves an historical overview of the
chosen topic, with particular attention given to earlier related theories,
seminal works, and the identification of trends, themes or patterns in the
literature to date. Debates within the chosen research context are situated
and important issues for the literature review to explore are highlighted,
as are exemplary studies.

The purpose of a literature review is to discuss the relevance of existing
research to that of the proposed research project. As well as exploring
related literature on a topic area, a literature review is also undertaken to
investigate suitable methodology and methods for conducting the research.
A literature review of this type illustrates the strengths and appropriateness
of applying particular methods to illicit the data required while also
addressing the weaknesses often associated with employing such methods.
The process of conducting your literature review is considered as providing
the foundation for your study. The length and breadth of the review will be
tailored to the length and scope of the research project and elements of the
literature review may be relocated to other parts of the thesis in developing
the overall argument when you are further along in the research process.

WHAT DOES A LITERATURE REVIEW INVOLVE?

Conducting an effective literature review is all about having a well-
structured plan to follow. Once you have decided on your topic, you can
begin by searching literature for what is already known in your topic
area. According to MacNaughton, Rolfe, and Siraj-Blatchford (2010),
undertaking a literature review has three broad aims: first, to acquaint
yourself with what has already been researched in the chosen area;
second, to refine your research question(s) by gaining a sense of what
questions have already been investigated and thus to determine how
your intended research can add to the knowledge-base; and third, to
expose you to various research designs so you can uncover relationships
between research questions and data collection methods.

It is imperative that the literature review shows evidence of the depth
and breadth of your reading and understanding of the topic area, along
with your ability to assimilate information obtained from various sources
into an integrated whole. It is not possible or expected that you cover all
literature that relates to the topic area; instead, plan to examine what is
most relevant to your research and focus on the main findings, concepts,
issues and theories put forward. Consider how these findings and issues

link to your study. For example, what is the relationship of the literature to your study in its context? A literature review is where a researcher can demonstrate that they have ownership of the field and the discourses in which knowledge in the field is constructed. This means paying attention to the academic and discipline-specific discourses in which the literature review needs to be located.

Above all, a literature review needs to show critical aptitude and confidence. This means being able to effectively analyse others' research, ensuring that you have the 'knowledge to make informed, evidence-based judgements' (Greig, Taylor, & MacKay, 2007, p. 65). MacNaughton, Rolfe, and Siraj-Blatchford (2010, p. 22) suggest applying the following questions to assist in the organisation and summarising of the literature:

- What are the key arguments, themes and issues?
- How have these changed over time?
- How many writers have explored each of these themes and issues?
- What seem to be the main points of agreement and disagreement between different writers?
- How representative of the theme or issue is the material you intend to include?

Hart (2005) suggests that the following questions, which set the historical, economic, social and technological contexts of the phenomenon under study, are considered:

- What are the key theories, concepts and ideas?
- What are the epistemological and ontological grounds for the discipline?
- What are the main questions and problems that have been addressed to date?
- How is knowledge on the topic structured and organised?
- What are the origins and definitions of the topic?
- What are the political standpoints?
- What are the major issues and debates about the topic?
- What are the key sources?

Constructing a well-written and well-composed literature review can be difficult, especially if the topic area and literature is new to you, as the conceptual, contextual and empirical elements need attention to ensure a critical argument is presented. Yates (2005) maintains that it takes time and often a level of immersion to understand some of the 'research agendas and definitions of boundaries and appropriate approaches given complex problems' (p. 72). She suggests that assistance from supervisors, induction programs, or attending conferences can help to 'get a sense of the practices and agendas that are not always explicit in the writings, but that frame how the discussion develops' (p. 72).

WHERE DOES A REVIEW OF RESEARCH METHODS FIT?

What also needs to be conducted is a literature review of the research methods to be applied in your study. This review will, first, locate the research approach to be adopted, moving to a closer examination of the strengths of each method applied. The purpose of this review is to justify the choice of methodology and methods for the type of data that needs to be collected to answer your research question(s) or to prove or disprove the hypothesis. Along with pointing out the strengths and relationship of each method to your research question(s), you need to outline the weaknesses that have been levelled at each, demonstrating how these weaknesses will be accounted for in your own study.

A review of research methodology and methods is an important aspect of your study as it can add clarity and strength to your overall research design, as the following example illustrates. The 'Exploring pedagogy' study aimed to capture the pedagogy of student teachers to determine whether there had been a shift in practice due to undertaking further qualifications. An extensive literature search was conducted early on in the design stage of the project to locate how other studies had examined pedagogy and the success of each method that had been used. A number of different search terms were used to compile an extensive bank of studies which assisted the researchers to make an informed argument about which method(s) were most appropriate to apply in their study.

Another example is from a study where the views of young children about their own experiences of starting school were considered imperative to address the study's aims. In this case, a literature review was conducted to locate ways to include the voices of young children that were respectful and democratic in nature. The review helped inform how the children participated in the study.

HOW DO I IDENTIFY LITERATURE RELATED TO MY TOPIC?

Begin by writing a 'brief' outlining your topic and the area of interest, and then be guided by what you find in the literature to generate your research questions. For example, one study which focused on young children transitioning to school, entitled 'Outcomes and indicators of a positive start to school', had the following brief:

The aim of this research is to identify the outcomes of a positive transition to school for children, their families and educators, and to establish indicators and corresponding measures for these outcomes. The outcomes should reflect the intended impact of participating in transition activities or processes.

This 'brief' stated the focus and purpose of the study, which guided the literature search. It was clear from the outset that the focus needed to be on research around children transitioning to school from multiple perspectives, and what has been identified as 'positive' outcomes. Also needed was a review of any literature on establishing indicators and measures relating to transition or associated attributes.

With access to so many publications from around the world in varying formats through the World Wide Web, a good starting point is to determine what databases you can access and are fit for purpose. Your database access and research topic requirements are determined by the scope and frame of your research project. It is important to become familiar with using online databases, and the journal titles available within them, as it will make your searches easier to conduct and less time-consuming when you understand the scope of each database. When using electronic databases, check to see if they have an automatic alert system which will keep you informed of any new publications in your topic area as they become available. If you are a student or staff member at a university or institute, you will be able to contact your library staff and begin discussions about those databases suitable for your literature search.

It is recommended that you access refereed journals first as these are considered more reliable sources for presenting research findings. All articles published in refereed journals have been peer-reviewed before being accepted, which is a measure of quality. Within these quality journals try to locate articles that give a broad overview of the literature on the topic area as these will give you a good sense of what is already available research-wise. For example, if you are searching for the topic of children's transitions to formal schooling, look to see if there is a journal specifically set up for the topic you are studying. You may find that names of particular researchers begin to be a recurring theme within the publications so search the researchers themselves to see if they have published other works on the same topic. You will find that canvassing the literature sets off a chain reaction where one search provides you with leads to other publications and so on, particularly if you begin to look at the reference lists and bibliographies of the retrieved articles, and use these to guide future searches. The following list of sources, other than journal articles, can all add vital information to your literature review. Try searching:

- reports
- theses
- conference papers
- books

- websites
- government documents.

Early in the process of conducting your literature review you will need to set the parameters for the search as well as the search terminology. Decide on the following to guide your search:

- date range
- geographical location
- language
- literature type (for example, academic or popular culture).

Next, decisions about key words to begin searching databases need to be made. Key words can be refined as results begin to be generated from the database searches. Once it was decided that the search of the literature for the 'Outcomes and indicators of a positive start to school' project would be restricted to publications in the last five years and would include national and international literature, key words guided the search of databases. Key words such as early childhood (education), kindergarten, preschool, success, measurement and assessment, proved fruitful in the initial search. The approach to finding relevant literature for this project progressed as follows: a search for books using an electronic database, another search conducted via a digital thesis database and another through a reputable education publications database, alongside an update of the online literature using the bibliographic databases, and the reviewing of a previously constructed literature review into school transition developed for a government project to avoid duplication of items already reviewed.

Be prepared to put aside time to develop and refine your key words for your searches as often terms differ across settings, countries and sectors. The use of a thesaurus (either attached to a particular database or a more general one) is useful here to identify related words. A literature search to inform a study related to investigating student teachers' pedagogy (as described earlier in this chapter) was problematic due to the many uses of the key term 'pedagogy'. Instead of identifying research related to student teacher pedagogy, what was uncovered was literature about teaching student teachers. In this case, the mid-career researcher conducting the literature review, Karina, began to formulate questions that helped her to clarify the focus, thereby refining the process. She began asking herself 'If we are investigating student teachers' pedagogy, would assessment of the practicum (field-based experience placement) be relevant?' Karina also began searching using the terms 'early childhood education' (as the student teachers were training for an early childhood teaching qualification) and 'practicum', as she could see the potential for comparing and contrasting the ways student teachers were assessed, which appeared to fit with the project's need to 'examine and explore student teacher practice'.

The refining continued with Karina corresponding with other researchers on the team to help her think through other possible terms to narrow the focus for the review. The following correspondence from Karina illustrates the refining process involved in the project:

> Thanks for the reply to my question about the terms 'practicum' and 'assessment'. I have spent some time this morning following up your suggestions to use 'practice' and 'education and training' and this (while not especially fruitful in itself) proved to be a valuable springboard to experimentation with other terms such as 'field experience' and 'pre-service teachers'. In the end I found 'teacher education' and 'assessment' to be promising, so I would just like to check this out with you. I think the broadening out of the search terms has been productive: any further suggestions would be welcome. It looks to me as if I will be using varied terms and approaches in the literature search.

One week later, Karina replied:

> After our email exchange about appropriate search terms for the review I pursued the idea of problematising the task and posed three questions:
>
> - Which research methods have been used to study student teachers?
> - How have changes in teaching behaviour/style been examined and analysed?
> - What approaches have been taken to study pedagogy?
>
> I have been able to collect a reasonable set of papers for the first two questions, however the third looks a little thin. I would appreciate your opinion on this.

Due to a lack of publications in your chosen topic area, you may find that you need to broaden your search by widening the scope of the search to include related fields. You will also need to decide if you intend to be selective or comprehensive in your coverage of the literature. Amy grappled with this complex issue, as can be seen in her reflections on this aspect of her research journey:

> I approached my literature review with trepidation… I immersed myself in readings about… well, there's not a lot on early giftedness so I had to go off on tangents – infant cognition studies and things about early intellectual development, analogical reasoning, metacognition, and scaffolding. I used the Vygotskian approach. I was looking at the Zone of Proximal Development, so a lot was on that. I had to go farther afield and try and make links to gifted development.

I had to create those links, and then also on research approaches, and because I did a quantitative study I had to tackle some fairly heavy statistical readings which I didn't quite understand a lot of the time. I suppose I felt that that was the way I would go (quantitative) simply because a lot of the literature that I was working with used that approach. Most of the research on early giftedness is more qualitative and I felt that I would make a better contribution if I went for something quantitative.

When discussing surprising elements about previous studies conducted in the area, Amy commented:

There was one study – The Fullerton Longitudinal Study [Gottfried, Eskeles Gottfried, Bathurst & Wright Guerin, 1994] – which I really got into and I actually used some aspects of their design for my study. That was a really good example of what should be happening because it was very thorough and longitudinal. And so the rest of the literature, while I found it very interesting, it did tend to be very personal and subjective. But I was also surprised because I had to look at a lot of the play literature – how little there is in the general literature on children's development, especially on advanced development. Nobody had ever really looked at advanced play development, though you could see in some of the studies that there had to be a couple of child participants who were way ahead – above the norms – nobody had explored it further.

We can see from the above that Amy's chosen methods for her research were very much influenced by the research studies outlined in the related literature. Amy also talks about the process of 'going off on a tangent' to find related literature on early giftedness before coming back to the original topic area. This illustrates that as a researcher, she was the person who needed to make the links between different bodies of literature, and it was not a straightforward process where a search on one topic uncovered all the literature needed for the review.

HOW DO I MANAGE THE MATERIAL AND WHEN DO I CONCLUDE A REVIEW?

Being organised and having a system in place is the key to managing the material accumulated by a literature search. You need to be able to access material when you need it, easily and efficiently, so locating it in logical places is important. For example, some researchers create special computer files where material on sub-topics within the main topic are filed. One researcher, Christine, used a dedicated filing cabinet in conjunction with a box file to store hard copies of materials. The filing cabinet was set up alphabetically according to author surnames and the box file contained a separate card for each publication with the reference details, key words, and a few sentences outlining the main points of the article. In this respect, the box file became a sort of annotated bibliography.

Some researchers find it useful to construct a literature trail which tracks the development of specific ideas or theories from article to article. It is best to note the material (author and details of an article), the main points proposed in the article, and follow the thread to other research studies mentioned within this initial article. By working in this way, you can follow the development and growth of the issues raised from the original idea. Exploring how theories or understandings about a topic have developed over time is a strength of this method of data management. It effectively tracks the course you take through the literature, drawing links across the materials you have accessed.

Whichever system you adopt or develop, it is certainly worth investing time into finding one that works for you, particularly as the amount of material you will accumulate can be significant. It is also worth ensuring that you have correctly referenced all sources, as it can take up valuable time in the final stages of the research if you have not sourced literature correctly the first time. There are software programs on the market that provide tools for managing and publishing reference lists and bibliographies which can be invaluable aids for researchers. The following experience of one novice researcher, Garrath, illustrates the importance of this.

> When it came to the end of my thesis I had 30 pages of references although there were a few that I had used that I had not recorded details for. It took me three weeks of intensive searching and then in the end I had to delete three references from the thesis itself as I just could not find the original source in time.

Determining the point at which to conclude your literature search is a decision that every researcher has to make. As Christine noted:

> At one point in my study I was concerned as to when to conclude reviewing the literature. I kept reading in fear that perhaps something just being produced would be significant to the study and I may miss out on it. After continuing to search the literature for a period of time and not uncovering anything new I decided it was time to stop. I therefore concluded reviewing the literature confident that I had developed a good understanding of the research that had been conducted and the issues raised by these studies.

This account by Christine gives a good justification of when to stop. However, until the research is concluded, always consider the literature review as a 'work in progress', as you may have to return to it once you have collected and analysed your findings to ensure that it does link strongly to your findings and discussion of these findings. On some occasions you may have to add a few more materials to the review or tailor what you have already included to improve the relevance or synergies with your data.

HOW DO I EVALUATE AND CRITIQUE THE RESEARCH LITERATURE?

There is no doubt that the quality of the literature you collate will vary. It is therefore essential that you make critical judgements on the value and worth of the materials. Clough and Nutbrown (2007) suggest that you undertake a 'radical reading' process, which involves asking yourself questions relating to the argument of the author, the audience of the piece, the aim, the evidence presented and how this compares with your own understanding of the topic. Your judgements will be based on the validity of what is presented. For example, if you choose articles from peer-reviewed journals, you can be reasonably assured that these have already been checked for quality and validity. You may find the following questions useful in the process of evaluating literature:

- Is the source reliable, valid and authoritative?
- Is the article or report logical in how it has been structured? That is, do all sections fit together with no inconsistencies? And does it make sense?
- Are the variables in the research clearly articulated?
- Are there gaps in the discussion of the findings? Are these mentioned?
- Is there internal validity? For example, were the procedures, analysis and conclusions appropriate and adequate enough to inform you of what took place?
- Was there any bias evident? Is this bias addressed in the study?
- Is there external validity? For example, is there any mention of how representative and generalisable the results are?
- Is this relevant to your topic?

Working through questions such as these will provide you with a framework to make informed judgements about the strength of the literature. Be aware that including literature that is unsubstantiated or incomplete might weaken the overall review and may detract from the overall robustness of your research project.

HOW DO I PRESENT A REVIEW?

It is best that you do not wait until you feel that you have read all there is to read on the topic before writing (see Lara's story, which follows, to gain a sense of how she tackled this). Instead, begin writing as soon as you begin reviewing the literature. If you have organised your materials under sub-headings, begin summarising these into themes or sub-topics. Begin by summarising the main argument or issue of each piece and how it relates to your topic. It is recommended that you write in prose rather than bullet points because then you have a starting point to begin shaping your literature review. In addition, you may be able to use some of these early sections in your final review.

The following excerpt, taken from a conversation with Lara about her research journey, provides a very graphic account of how she undertook her literature review:

> I suppose with my topic area, 'An investigation exploring the experiences of a range of practitioners using graphic symbols with children in Foundation Stage (3–5 years) school settings', being an exploratory area, there was a bit of literature about collaborative practice and special needs or specific technology or something like that, but there wasn't any about just the use of symbols. So what I did was try to take three or four really key areas of the literature that were separate and have a look at whether there was any overlap between those areas and, if there wasn't, then that clearly identified my research as an exploratory topic. Those would probably have been 'augmentative and alternative communication', which was where most of the symbol literature resides, and 'inter-professional education, inter-professional practice' as another area of the literature. I then got into symbolic development and what we're actually asking or expecting children to do when we use symbols with them, especially in that young age group. I also had to consider other areas of literature as well, such as special needs education and pedagogy, approaches to education, and so on. So I really just gave an overview of each of those areas of literature with any focus on any overlaps, no matter how limited they were, and identified a clear gap.

In the following dialogue Lara focuses on how she set herself criteria to help manage the process:

> I had my search terms and it was a long list. I did have inclusion and exclusion criteria in terms of years and so on, and relevance, but I didn't really focus on, for example, the number of random controlled trials. What I did was tabulate the papers that I found, and I tabulated them by the kind of research topic that they were under, and then a bit about what each study was about, what their findings were, who their participants were, what their methods were. Then I inter-rated it over three years, basically because obviously I came and went

from that literature review, and it was probably the last chapter that I was working on in the end. It needed a lot of polishing three and a half years later at the end of my study.

I did have a systematic approach to how I organised the review. You have to, especially if you're doing an exploratory topic. Where you're not looking at what's already been done, you have to identify what are the related areas, draw a line around those and get to know each of them. But, the risk with doing it that way is that you can go too far down one road, and if you are looking at something that's bringing new concepts together, you can't neglect any of them. They all need to be there. Being reflective helped me make that decision. I guess it's being reflexive, well, reflective and reflexive, which was part of my qualitative research process, which involved making a lot of notes, talking about it, and thinking it through. I would have a go at writing something as much as possible, even if it was just bullet points. An example is I would open up a file, call it 'Literature Review'. You know you're not really writing yet, but just write a few sentences. I did that for a few months before I put it into continuous prose. I mean, getting advice from other people as well, because I can remember my supervisor saying to me 'you will start to pick up papers and think "isn't it interesting?" but it's just not relevant'. And you know, you'll also find that you're halfway through reading something and you remember that you've already read it. Those little anecdotes from people were really useful as well.

At the end of her study, Lara refined her literature review as she explains:

I didn't replace the studies. I didn't really find many more, but what I realised when it got to really refining my thesis was that up until that very late stage I wasn't really writing the kind of literature review that would be required. It took me quite a few attempts with that chapter to learn how to make a point, refer to the papers, then, take the paper and explain what they did and why it's relevant within a relatively small word count. That was definitely a tough chapter.

For beginning researchers, Lara offers the following advice:

I think, just make a start, and just see it for what it is, which is the intensive period of reading and generating more reading, and reading through of that and generating more reading. And I mean I can remember when I started reading a paper [journal articles] and for every paper I read identifying ten more papers and thinking 'how am I ever going to read these papers?' The other side of that for me was that keeping the papers was really useful. Keeping the papers in files as I cannot say how many times I went back to them because I wanted to quote them or I hadn't written down the end page number. Just having them to go back over what they'd said... so I know it's not environmentally friendly but I needed to have the papers. You do need to look at them again.

Lara shows how the process of conducting a literature review undergoes several stages, including finding relevant literature to review and clearly demarcating which topic areas are to be pursued. This is not such an easy task, as Lara discovered, when the topic area being studied is exploratory or a new aspect of a topic. Even when she thought her literature review was almost complete, Lara realised that it still required further development and editing to ensure that it was presented in the way that was expected at a doctoral level.

Determining the most appropriate format to use when setting out the review will depend on the purpose of the research – for example, whether it is a thesis, a contracted government report or another type of study – and there could be a preferred style. A comprehensive literature review will usually divide the topic into important themes and then address each theme under sub-headings. For clarity purposes, ensure that there are enough written signposts for the reader. This ensures that the reader is able to logically navigate his/her way through the review, emerging with a more informed understanding of the topic under investigation and how the body of knowledge has synergies with your project. You may also find it relevant to move some elements of your review to other sections of your thesis, for example to the discussion section, to strengthen your overall argument.

A literature review should begin with an introduction to the topic. To 'set the scene' you will need to note the significance and importance of the topic and demonstrate that your review will provide a comprehensive coverage of the key concepts, issues and themes. You may be able to resolve theoretical and/or empirical problems in the review. Ensure that seminal studies, as recognised by the field or discipline, are included as these show your ability to understand the area and help to contextualise your study. Demonstrate the links between the literature you have collected and other related knowledge domains to show that you understand the complexity of the topic. Gaps or omissions from the literature, along with any conflicting views or theories and any areas of debate, also need to be outlined. Clear arguments need to be developed within the major issues, areas or themes. By organising the review under logical themes that relate to your questions, and providing critical and evaluative reflections of the literature, you guarantee that the literature review stays relevant to the research project. The conclusion of the review should summarise the important points raised and highlight the synergies these have with your own research. 'A good literature review will leave the reader convinced that there are unexplained areas and problems associated with the issue, and agree with your assessment that further research is needed' (Kervin, Vialle, Herrington, & Okely, 2006, p. 50).

It is best to avoid unconvincing, unsupported, purely descriptive, isolated, fragmented, incoherent, poorly informed statements. Overall, make sure it is logical in presentation, is succinct and challenging, and comes together as an integrated, coherent whole. As Yates (2005, pp. 71–72) points out in relation to theses under examination:

> The literature review, for example, is not merely there to show that the writer has done some background reading, but to set up *what type of a thesis* this is; to show which discussions he or she is aiming to make a contribution to. A good discussion of the field sets up a story of why the particular topic of the thesis matters, as well as why it is appropriate to embark on it in such a way.

The discussion that Yates refers to here is the one that you develop within the literature review itself.

REFLECTION POINTS

When reviewing the literature, the following questions will help guide you in the process:

- What has been published on this topic within the parameters I have set?
- What is the historical overview of this topic?
- What are regarded as the seminal works?
- What are the identified trends, themes or patterns?
- What are the contested or debated areas related to this topic?
- What are the gaps or omissions, if any, from previous research?
- Which questions still remain unanswered?
- What are the links or synergies to my research project?

☐ Summary

The focus of this chapter was on preparing a comprehensive literature review, ensuring it provides the reader with a more informed, critical understanding of the topic under investigation and how this body of knowledge has synergies with the research project. It has drawn attention to:

- deciding on parameters for the search;
- developing a system to manage the material; and
- setting out the review in an appropriate manner.

6

GUIDING THE RESEARCH JOURNEY: ETHICAL CONSIDERATIONS

This chapter discusses what needs to be considered when conducting social research, especially when the research involves young children.

Key chapter questions are:

- What do I need to know to ensure I act in a responsible way?
- What does being ethical mean in research?
- How do I gain informed consent from participants?
- How do I deal with existing power relations?
- How are judgements made about the ethical nature of research?
- What ethical considerations are needed when the research involves young children?

  - children's involvement in research
  - acknowledging children's rights and giving them choice
  - capturing children's voices

WHAT DO I NEED TO KNOW TO ENSURE I ACT IN A RESPONSIBLE WAY?

A researcher commits to a range of responsibilities when they decide to undertake research. All research involves ethical decisions which become even more complex when young children are involved in some capacity in the research process. By its very nature, research in the social sciences is problematic as you deal with people and places that impact the lives of those involved, either directly or indirectly. Even though you may be very curious and keen to get started on your research journey, how you access the places and people who will become the focus on your research needs thoughtful consideration. Foremost is that care needs to be taken to ensure that the site and the participants are able to be recruited in an ethical manner. As a responsible researcher you need to afford your participants the following considerations:

- that they will be fully informed of the research process before making a decision on their involvement;
- that participation is voluntary (they have the right to withdraw without penalty or any ill-effects);
- that different views about the issue/topic are appreciated;
- that different cultures and values will be acknowledged in a respectful way;
- that the diverse needs of participants will be addressed;
- that participants' rights will be upheld;
- that information will be treated confidentially.

When children are involved in the research, the responsibilities also include adhering to a set of principles such as:

- understanding and believing in the importance of giving children a say in decisions that affect them;
- having realistic expectations about participation and how long it will last;
- making sure that children understand their role in the process;
- ensuring that children find the experience enjoyable and rewarding (as much as possible);
- informing children of the research findings (reporting back to them in a way that is understandable to them).

Children should be afforded the same rights and respect that you would give adult participants. Even very young children can be involved as participants in research projects if you ensure that the participation method(s) are suitable for the children involved. Throughout this book you will find more specific details about a range of techniques and strategies for involving children in research in an ethical, reciprocal and responsive way.

WHAT DOES BEING ETHICAL MEAN IN RESEARCH?

In research, one automatically has power over the research process and the participants. The researcher shapes the research and decides who, what, when, where, why and how (see Chapter 4). This means that the researcher takes on certain roles and responsibilities in the process and must be mindful of the impact these have on the participants and the settings – from the research design, through to publication of the research findings. Sensitivity and respect is called for as settings are located and participants are invited to participate. Trust needs to be built between the researcher and the potential participants and gatekeepers so they gain a sense that it will not be detrimental to them to participate in the research. Kiara, a Master's student who at the time of her study was also working full-time in the early childhood field, discussed with her supervisor her conscious decision to locate her own voice within her study and her positioning:

> I wanted to write using 'I' as I find it important in this study to locate my 'voice' in the research, considering my own involvement with the early childhood field for over twenty years. Hopefully, in my completed report I have achieved my aim and have produced a representational account where my voice is located in relation to the voices of other participants. I have chosen to make use of the 'confessional style', as defined by Van Maanen (1988), when considering my influence within the study.

'Confessions' are seen as valuable. As in Kiara's study, they make readers aware of the researcher's biases and the assumptions he/she holds about the nature of learners and learning. Who the researcher is impacts on all aspects of the research process and therefore must be noted. Locating yourself within the study is one way of disclosing any personal biases that would otherwise go unnoticed and could skew the data analysis and interpretations. Having a vested interest or being an 'insider' to the situation needs to be clearly acknowledged in any research reports to enable the audience to judge the interpretations in an informed way.

To begin this process, the researcher must be upfront to all concerned about the aim(s) of the research project and what involvement entails. Prospective participants need detailed information to be provided in a form they can understand in order to make any informed decision as to whether or not to participate. Ethics committees of any organisations involved will need to be contacted before any research project can begin, and the research proposal will be examined on its ethical merit. These ethics committees, embedded within organisations such as universities, government departments and local authorities, usually require researchers to submit a completed template for consideration before the go-ahead is given to the proposed research project. These templates require you to outline details such as:

- the title of the project;
- the names of the researchers;
- the type of project (whether it is a student project or a funded or non-funded project);
- a brief description of the project, including the aims and methodology and methods to be applied;
- details of the participants and how they will be invited to participate and what they will be asked to do;

- the proposed dates when the project will be undertaken;
- an indication if approval is required from other organisations for the research to progress.

You will also be required to provide responses relating to the intrusiveness of the project, such as using physically intrusive techniques, causing discomfort in participants beyond normal levels of inconvenience, covering potentially sensitive or contentious areas, using therapeutic techniques or seeking disclosure of information which may be prejudicial to participants. You will need to outline whether or not you will be seeking personal information from a government agency, if the project involves deception or covert observation, and if there is a conflict of interest between any of the researchers and potential participants in the research – for example, a relationship between the researcher and the participant population.

   Issues surrounding confidentiality must also be addressed. For example, you will need to summarise the procedures undertaken to ensure confidentiality, naming who will be responsible for the security of confidential data collected during the research project and how it will be stored, the length of time the data will be held and who will have access to it during that time, as well as how the data will be destroyed at the end of the nominated period. Also required are details relating to the potential risks of the research project and the proposed procedures to be undertaken, such as physical, psychological, social, legal and any other perceived risks. If any risks are identified, it must be explained how these will be dealt with, minimised and/or managed if they occur. This is known as a risk analysis.

HOW DO I GAIN INFORMED CONSENT FROM PARTICIPANTS?

For any research project, informed consent must be acquired from participants. As part of the informed consent process it is necessary to provide the potential participants with information about the research project prior to asking them to consent to participate. This information usually takes the form of an information sheet, which is often referred to as a Plain Language Statement (as it must be written in plain language and easily understood). For participants where English is not their first language, this information should be translated into their home language or communicated via an interpreter. The information sheet explains to the potential participant or organisation as openly and clearly as possible all the procedures involved in the project so that they can make a fully informed decision as to whether they are going to participate or allow their staff to be invited to participate. It is good practice to encourage potential participants to discuss the project with others, outside of the project, before making a decision. Also noted in the information provided are the purpose and background of the study, along with the overall aims and procedures that participants will be involved in, indicating the possible benefits and any risks associated with being involved. Some studies, while having no immediate benefits to the participants, do hold the potential to make a positive contribution to something, for example adding to the related literature, informing policy, or promoting changes to practice or changes to training programs. Mukherji and Albon (2010) make the point that 'people are often happy to participate in a piece of research, especially if they are confident that you have their best interests at heart and that in some way their participation will make a positive contribution to something they view as important' (p. 39).

Privacy, confidentiality and disclosure of information are addressed in the information provided to potential participants, along with the plan for dissemination of the findings. It must be clearly noted on the information sheet that participation is voluntary and some clause written about how choosing to participate or not will not impact on the current or future relationships with the researcher or institution/organisation the researcher is from.

Choosing to participate and then changing one's mind will need careful consideration because in some cases, after a certain point in a project, it is impossible to remove specific data. This needs to be detailed in the information provided to potential participants, including information about the revocation of consent. An example of this is taken from a project that explored how resilience is learnt and practised by young people between the ages of 5 and 19 years. The mixed methods employed in this longitudinal study consisted of interviews, observations, surveys, audits and social networking maps. It was made clear to the potential adult participants that if they wanted to withdraw within the four weeks following the interview, any information obtained from them would not be used. It was noted that after that time data would be transcribed, anonymised (using pseudonyms) and aggregated, which meant it could no longer be identified and separated out from the complete data set. Working in this way, the potential participants knew the parameters of their participation before making a decision to be involved.

A contact for complaints about any aspect of the project, the way it is conducted or any questions relating to the participants' rights will need to be included, along with researchers' names and contact details should further information be required. This information should be written in language which is readily understood by members of the general public and any technical terms should be explained.

A consent form for signing by potential participants should accompany the information sheet. However, in some instances participants will not be asked to sign a consent form. In cases where an anonymous survey is being used, participants can be made aware (via the information sheet) that by completing and returning the survey they are giving consent for their responses to be incorporated into the research data. If children are the focus of the project, it is their parents or legal guardians who are asked to sign the consent form. However, asking children directly if they are comfortable with participating should accompany the parental consent process. This will be discussed in more detail later in this chapter. It is also important to make it clear to the parent or guardian what level of consent you are asking for and they are agreeing to. For example, in a large-scale longitudinal study that aimed to identify a number of factors (the role of the teacher, home-life and child characteristics that were positively associated with positive outcomes in literacy in the first year of school), parents were able to choose the level of consent for their child. Some parents allowed their child to be part of the research project (interviewed, observed and tested), but not included in the video footage. Others chose to allow filming of their child in the early childhood setting, deciding whether the images could be used on a publically available website as part of the 'products' of the research project or for teaching purposes only.

HOW DO I DEAL WITH EXISTING POWER RELATIONS?

When a researcher has an established relationship with potential participants (for example, a teacher and her students or a health worker and a client), then the nature of this relationship will need further explaining before ethical approval can be granted. This is to ensure that the potential participants don't feel obliged or coerced into participation. The following two examples detail projects where the researchers held power over the participants due to their professional positions and the implications each had on the ethical processes.

Example 1: Examining experiential learning: the Kinda Kinder experience

In this research project a group of university lecturers wanted to research the learning of their pre-service early childhood teachers. The research was designed to identify and document the student teacher experience of participating in the Kinda Kinder program. This program involved experiential learning where pre-service early childhood teachers and vocational education childcare students worked together with mentors, university colleagues and communities in the development, implementation and evaluation of supported playgroups located in community settings. The focus of the project was on whether this type of experiential learning situation conformed or transformed the practice of the pre-service teachers. It was decided that learning and knowledge construction and transmission needed to be explored in this context from the perspective of the student teachers. The data collection methods included in this qualitative study were surveys, interviews, artefacts (selected extracts from student teacher journals) and a case study that allowed a more in-depth study of one student teacher's experience.

From an ethical perspective, attention in this project needed to be focused on the power relations that existed between the researchers (the university lecturers) and the participants (the student teachers whom the lecturers taught on the courses). The risks were both psychological – the student teachers may have been anxious that their participation or non-participation may have affected their academic results – and social risks – there may have been an impact on the quality of the student teachers relationship with staff and other students. In this situation it was important that it was made clear to the ethics committee how these identified risks were to be minimised. The following extract from the ethics application for the project demonstrates how this was addressed:

> Even though some participants are students of members of the research team, responses to the survey are anonymous, as is the voluntary submission of excerpts from the Reflective Journals. As such, this should minimise the risk. Students who volunteer to undertake an interview will be allocated a pseudonym in any publications arising from the research. Interviewees will have an opportunity to read the interview transcript and add or detract comments. Once they have agreed on the accuracy of the interview transcript, their identifying details will be removed so that from that point on the interview data will not be able to be traced back to the individual who provided it. The Research Team will ensure that a team member who does not assess the work of the student to be interviewed conducts the interview. All interviews will be held after the submission of assessment tasks for the units the students are studying.

Even though this research project was deemed as low risk, as the participants were reflecting on and exploring their understandings of their own learning during the Kinda Kinder program (which is a common practice within teacher education courses), the issues surrounding the power relations needed further thought and articulation to ensure that the student teachers did not feel obliged to participate or give responses that would be regarded as what the lecturers wanted to hear. This is addressing the issue of consent without coercion.

Example 2: Exploring the research process: perspectives from the inside

The aim of this study was to capture the experiences of those involved in conducting research in early childhood. It explored participants' understandings, struggles and successes of the complex issues raised when researching in the early childhood sector. It endeavoured to capture the practical and ethical issues of researching with young children that researchers face so that these could be shared with others contemplating researching in this area. Eight to ten participants were to be selected on the basis that they were known to the researchers and had completed or were currently completing research in the early childhood field. An additional criterion was that some of the researchers were applying methodologies that had not been previously used in early childhood research.

Potential participants included current students (but not students for whom the researchers had direct responsibility), former students of the researchers, colleagues, as well as current and former research partners. Again, due to the issue of power relations, it was necessary to add a clause to the ethics application illustrating the fact that former students were being recruited due to the low number of potential participants in the field of early childhood research. It was also noted that this could have had an effect on the quality of the data, although this was counterbalanced by a reassurance that if they did decide to participate (and there was no obligation to participate) they would be provided with the opportunity to remain anonymous and would be allocated a pseudonym in any publications arising from the research. It was also made clear to the potential participants that they were under no obligation to participate and that their decision whether to participate or not would not impact on the relationship already established with the researchers.

Both of these examples outline issues of power relations between the researcher and the participants as in both cases the researchers were researching their students. This type of research is often labelled 'insider' research and involves the consideration of complex ethical issues. As Anning (2010) suggests, these revolve around the dual role of being both a professional and a researcher within the setting. 'The brutal fact is that your position as a professional gives you power over your community; but is it justifiable to use this power as a researcher as well without serious thought and preparation?' (Anning, 2010, p. 190). Anning questions whether this is morally and ethically defensible. This type of research has been shown to be useful in impacting practice and 'everyday' issues that arise within settings, so rather than dismissing this as too difficult from an ethical and moral stance, time needs to be invested to ensure that all key stakeholders are fully informed and comfortable with the proposed research process and that ethical issues are addressed.

HOW ARE JUDGEMENTS MADE ABOUT THE ETHICAL NATURE OF RESEARCH?

Ethics committees consider the research proposal in terms of the implications and benefits of the research to the clients/participants and the impact of the research on the field in general. These committees usually meet regularly and the results of the review are communicated to the researcher soon after the meeting. Research proposals must comply with all relevant privacy legislation. For example, researchers in Victoria, Australia, have to comply with the Australia Privacy Act 1988 (Commonwealth), the Information Privacy Act 2000 (Victoria) and the Health Records Act 2001 (Victoria). With a favourable outcome from the ethics committee comes responsibilities for the researcher, such as keeping the committee informed of any changes to the research project if and when they occur, providing reports (at intervals determined by the committee throughout the project or at least a final report or summary), and the opportunity for comment on any publication arising from the research.

If the research focuses on what are considered 'at risk' or potentially 'vulnerable' groups, a more elaborate ethical process will need to be undertaken to ensure that these groups are not disadvantaged by the research process. These groups are usually nominated as including children under the age of 18 years, Indigenous groups, people in dependent or unequal relationships, those who are highly dependent on medical care, those who are cognitively or intellectually impaired or those who are involved in illegal activities. When gaining ethical approval for research involving children (from birth to 18 years of age) there are specific ethical processes that are required which act to safeguard children from harmful practice. An example of this is how university ethics committees, erring on the conservative side, do not consider applications involving children to be low risk research projects, and as a consequence these applications have to go through a rigorous ethical process.

Another way to consider the ethics of research is to apply a framework, such as the Ethical Response Cycle (Newman & Pollnitz, 2002). Developed in response to concerns within the early childhood field, Newman and Pollnitz suggest that this framework 'represents a process that helps professionals to apply and justify sensitive and intelligent reasoning to problematic situations' (2002, p. 111). This was developed for tertiary educators, student teachers and professionals working in the early childhood field and is a useful tool to assist in thinking through aspects of early childhood research from an ethical standpoint. The framework consists of the following aspects and subsequent actions:

- Legal aspects – 'checking for enforceable legal factors including national laws; state laws/regulations; system regulations/codes; employer regulations/codes' (Newman & Pollnitz, 2002, p. 115).
- Professional considerations – referring 'to core values; codes of ethics; principles of professional practice; policies and guidelines' (p. 115).
- Ethical theories – drawing on philosophical positions such as:

    - Rule-based: 'moral obligations to adhere to religious or societal regulations' (p. 115);
    - Ends-based: 'obligation to make judgements that result in the greatest good for the greatest number of people' (p. 115);
    - Proportion-based: 'obligation to make judgements that are underpinned by systematic and intelligent/rational thought processes and take the specific circumstances into account' (p. 115); and
    - Care-based: 'obligation to make judgements that are situation sensitive and are underpinned by consideration of maintenance of nurturing and caring human relationships' (p. 115).

- Informed inclination – drawing 'on professional dispositions; knowledge; expertise; extended experience' (p. 115).
- Judgement – making 'judgements that are the outcome of a well-considered reasoning process; can be justified; form the basis for a sound ethical response' (p. 115).
- Action – taking 'appropriate action as dictated by the judgement' (p. 115).
- Documentation – recording 'detailed information about the process of arriving at the judgement; the proposed and actual action; any implications for further action; developments arising in the aftermath of the judgement' (p. 115).
- Reflection – critically evaluating 'the outcome of the judgement and action to determine if the resolution is complete or requires further consideration; the implementation of the 'Ethical Response Cycle' for future reference; the development of own competence to resolve dilemmas' (p. 115).

WHAT ETHICAL CONSIDERATIONS ARE NEEDED WHEN THE RESEARCH INVOLVES YOUNG CHILDREN?

Children's involvement in research

Matters that have a direct impact on children should see them included in the research process, but this calls for ethical considerations of how they can best be represented in the research and have their 'voices' legitimated in the data. The challenge of involving children in research is described by Cartmel (personal correspondence, 2010) as follows:

> Researching with children has its own particular challenges and researchers need to be mindful of the kinds of consent and the kinds of different strategies that we can use to engage with children so that the adult's perspective is not given the priority – the methodologies allow the children to explore and explain their perspectives.

There are different ways in which children can be involved in research. Kellett (2010) acknowledges four typologies, including: research on children, research about children, research with children, and research by children. It is this last category that is perhaps the most contentious as Kellett (2010, p. 22) explains:

> Research by children goes a step further than children as participants or co-researchers. Children are empowered to lead their own research, set their own agendas, decide the topics that are important to research, choose the methods to employ and actively engage in analysis and dissemination of their own findings.

What is apparent is that whichever typology is chosen, any research with children, rather than on children, brings with it a unique set of ethical considerations. For example, Rasmusson (2011) discovered that researching with children and families who had experienced child protection and were known to the police was possible if certain conditions were met. These were the establishment of a friendly, safe environment where interviews could take place, kind treatment by staff, the fact that the interviewer was a person with whom the participants already had an established relationship, and that participants had all finished their connections with the professionals and the organisation.

Researchers such as Dockett and Einarsdottir (2010) point to the importance of finding ethical ways to involve children as genuine partners in the research and, in relation to the research process, ask researchers to consider the following questions:

- Do children get to choose whether or not they participate?
- What information is available to them?
- How do they understand the consequences of participation or non-participation?
- Is there a chance to review their decision?
- How easy is it for a child or children to say 'no'?
- If the research is representative, do children get to decide who represents them?
- How does the research acknowledge the diversity of children?
- Is it expected that some children will be silent? How will this decision be respected?
- Who chooses the research locations or familiar settings? Do the children have some control in the settings?
- How does the research invade the children's private spaces?
- Does the research contribute to the increased surveillance of children's lives and experiences?
- How does the researcher respect the trust given by the child or children?
- Who owns the data?
- How is it to be shared with the children?
- How can this be negotiated with the children?

The answers to these important questions determine the positioning of children and the ethical stance taken by the researcher.

Acknowledging children's rights and giving them choice

As has been mentioned elsewhere in this book, it is extremely important that any research involving children is constructed from a rights perspective (Kellett, 2010). Viewing children in this way positions them as competent persons in their own right who hold expertise about their own lives and who are able to share this knowledge with others. The research community now embraces the agency of young children and accepts their capabilities of being able to process information relating to their everyday lives.

Children's perspectives should be considered as a critical component of the research design, influencing all aspects of the research process. We, the authors, hold the belief that every child, no matter what their age or ability, should have the opportunity to decide whether they wish to participate or not. This means that they need the project to be explained to them in ways that they can understand, positioning informed consent as 'a fundamental right of every child irrespective of age or ability' (Kellett, 2010, p. 24). Dockett and Perry (2011) see providing information to children about the project as more than a one-off activity. They embrace the idea that it is an ongoing process, giving children a chance to reassess their participation over the life of the project. This can mean reminding the child or children every time you enter the setting what you are doing and requesting their consent. Strategies suggested by Kellett (2010) to assist children to understand what is being asked of them go beyond the verbal explanations. These include the use of child-friendly leaflets, role-playing scenarios and drawings.

If the child is an infant and/or is non-verbal, giving consent can be somewhat more problematic and this is where watching their body language and responding to it in a responsive way shows respect for the intentions of the child. The work of Langston, Abbott, Lewis and Kellett (2004) demonstrates that very young children can give or withdraw their consent to participate by their body language. Behaviours such as turning away and crying, appearing distressed, becoming quieter than their usual demeanour, refusing to engage with the researcher or the materials from the research, are all indications that the young child does not wish to participate. These actions need to be respected, acknowledged and acted on by the researcher.

Capturing children's voices

Thought is needed when choosing the methodology to ensure that the understandings, ideas and opinions of children are represented in the way they were intended. It is important to ensure that children understand what is being asked of them in ways that they can identify with. This requires you, as the researcher, to design methods that will not disadvantage the child and will allow the child's perspective to be represented by the data rather than by the inferences of the researcher. It also means choosing data collection methods that help children to feel safe and supported in the research process.

Different studies employ different methods to obtain data, such as narrative approaches to uncover the perceived worlds of a group of children aged 6–12 years old (Gil & Jover, 2000), the use of an electronic survey to explore legal, ethical and pedagogical aspects of children's rights to education, and written stories and an in-depth, open biographical interview accompanied by drawings for the younger children (aged 6–9 years) to capture the children's views of their world now and into the future (Jover & Thoilliez, 2011). An undergraduate student, Amber, was collecting data from children as part of a project while she was on field placement in an early childhood setting. Amber decided to use phenomenology as the research methodology and then chose multiple methods to collect her data from the children. The methods included using a combination of interviews and visual methods, such as drawing and mind-mapping (a nonlinear, graphical representation of information around a particular topic or concept) (Jackson, 2009). Having the children draw reduced children's eye contact with her which hopefully made them feel more comfortable to share their ideas, while providing a greater sense of control over the research process (Dockett & Perry, 2007). By then discussing the drawings with the child, any misinterpretation was avoided (Swadener, 2005; Veale, 2005). By using multiple methods of data collection, children's interest in the research can be stimulated, and the likelihood of accessing their true perspective of an experience enhanced (Green & Hill, 2005).

Mackey and Vaealiki (2011) conducted a case study looking at young children's involvement in a kindergarten environmental education program using a research approach that developed trusting relationships and respectful forms of communication built on the notion of democratic participation. They wanted to allow children's voices to be heard and their contribution to the research project to be valued. By 'developing a research process that respected the rights of children and families and provided a range of ways for them to participate', they were able to achieve this (Mackey & Vaealiki, 2011, p. 82). The researchers wrote a letter to the children explaining the research project and asked parents to read the letter to their child. They also provided an information sheet about the project to enable parents and teachers to answer children's questions. Site visits and immersing themselves in the culture of the setting over a significant period of time allowed the children to become more familiar with the researchers. Working in this way also allowed the researchers to develop a better understanding of the differing ways that the children expressed their thoughts, such as engaging in conversation rather than posing questions, and enabled them to detail a thoughtful and respectful exit plan as a way of formally concluding the data collection period. Mackey and Vaealiki (2011) ask other researchers to question: 'How are children afforded the opportunities to comment or give an opinion about their participation and learning through experience in their communities?' (p. 83).

As Jover and Thoilliez (2011) conclude, after undertaking a suite of studies focusing on listening to children's voices over a 12-year period, where attention was paid to the process as well as the outcomes, listening to children's voices can be justified from epistemological, ethical and pedagogical perspectives. As proclaimed in the United Nations Convention on the Rights of the Child (1989), children have the right to quality research about their childhood, to which we would add – and the right to be involved in that research in an ethical and respectful way.

REFLECTION POINTS

When considering your research work from an ethical standpoint, we hope the following questions will be useful in guiding your thinking:

- What are the ethical processes that I need to undertake for my project?
- How can I ensure that I build trusting, professional relationships with potential participants and organisations?
- What are the issues that I face in my research project that I need to be aware of concerning the principle of informed consent?
- How do I feel about involving children in research?
- How do I position children within the research?

  - Do I acknowledge children as active citizens with rights?
  - Have I positioned children as participants or co-researchers?
  - Do I see children as taking an active role in the research process?

- How can I include the 'voices' of children in authentic and legitimate ways?

▢ Summary

This chapter has discussed the importance of researchers working within an ethical framework, especially when the research involves young children. It has highlighted considerations related to:

- the ethical decisions needing to be considered when designing research;
- issues surrounding informed consent; and
- power differentials between the researcher and the researched and what this means to being ethical.

7

MOVING ALONG QUALITATIVE METHODOLOGICAL PATHWAYS

This chapter introduces readers to qualitative research methodologies and methods, and the characteristics associated with conducting this type of research. Researchers who are seeking to understand complex or diverse human circumstances tend to favour using qualitative methods rather than quantitative methods, which usually involve some form of experimental control or statistics. Subsequently, the next chapter focuses on quantitative methodology and methods.

Undertaking qualitative research allows the focus to be more in-depth on smaller populations, capturing the experiences and the meanings attributed to these experiences by the participants, in a detailed and intimate way. The chapter includes references to qualitative research designs which encompass phenomenological inquiry, ethnographic methodology, historical research, case studies, action research, and policy analysis. Also discussed are some of the data-gathering tools, such as interviewing and focus groups, which are common to the various types of research designs. The implications of involving children in a more active role relating to qualitative data collection are also considered. Further, this chapter discusses data generated by the research designs and tools, focusing on the management of the information (data) process and the related traditions when handling and analysing research data. Lara's personal journey, relating to how she approached data analysis within her study, is included in this chapter.

Key chapter questions are:

- What are some qualitative research methodologies?
- What research methods can I choose?
- How are reliability and validity ensured when taking a qualitative approach to research?

- What do I need to consider when thinking about qualitative data analysis?
- How do I organise the data into a useable form to aid analysis?
- How do I code data?
- What are the different approaches to analysing qualitative data?
- What do I need to be mindful of if I want children to be more involved in the research process?

It is critical for a researcher to know what methodologies and methods are available to them so that they can design their project to answer their research questions. Qualitative research usually aligns with small-scale projects, where attention needs to be focused on the participants' experiences and the meaning they make of their experiences in a detailed way. Often conducted in naturalistic settings, this research approach captures personal experience through words and visual means, and the researcher's position in the research is acknowledged as it can be influential.

WHAT ARE SOME QUALITATIVE RESEARCH METHODOLOGIES?

There are some very well-tried qualitative methodologies, and associated methods, for addressing research questions. The selection of methodology and research methods is referred to as the research design (see Chapter 4). The design of your research needs to reflect the kind of questions you are trying to answer and the context in which you intend to collect your data. Once you have an idea of your research question(s), you can decide which methodology, plan of action, methods, techniques and procedures, will enable you to collect the type of data you will need to answer the question(s) (see Chapters 2, 3 and 4). This means deciding between taking a qualitative approach, a quantitative approach (which is discussed in the next chapter), or perhaps you will use both forms in a mixed method approach (also discussed in the next chapter).

Qualitative research methodologies are concerned with understanding individuals' perceptions of the world. The strength of the qualitative approach is the ability to focus on the critical and determining factors of the human element in the definition of truth and knowledge. However, due to the often subjective nature of the research methodology and methods, specific attention will need to be paid to ensuring adequate validity and reliability. There is not a clear process to help shape research designs because the interests, context and methodologies of the researchers all influence each other (see Chapter 2). Mason and Dale (2011) contend that this can sometimes be a conundrum for beginning researchers and that reading the stories of others, as contained in this book, can sometimes be very helpful for understanding the complexities of the research process. Some examples of qualitative research methodologies are:

- Phenomenological inquiry – a study of structures of experience, or consciousness from the first-person point of view;
- Ethnographic methodology – an examination of human social phenomena and communities, sometimes comparing and contrasting different cultures;
- Grounded theory – a process of generating a theory from systematically collecting data;
- Case studies – used to look at individuals, a small group of participants, a group, or an intervention, drawing conclusions only about that participant or group, or intervention, and only in that specific context;
- Action research – pursues action (or change) and research (or understanding) at the same time;
- Geneaology – reflects on current circumstances using descriptions of the interrelations of past practice and knowledge, particularly throwing into doubt current rules;
- Discourse analysis – in-depth, critical analysis of the social relations within data texts;
- Narrative inquiry – the study of experience as a story and a way of hearing people's stories with the intention of gaining knowledge from their lived experience (Clandinin & Connelly, 2000). Story is a portal through which experiences of the world are interpreted and made meaningful. Narrative inquiry can be used as the underpinning theoretical perspective as well as the research methodology.

Once you have chosen the methodology, it is important to select appropriate data collection methods. Lara's comments about her research journey, which follow, relate to her use of phenomenology as a methodology and offers some hints about the process of preparing for and collecting data.

> There are so many things to think about when you are choosing the methodology that best suits gathering the data that you need to explore in order to answer your research and that takes into consideration your own knowledge and experiences. I used phenomenology. I thought about using grounded theory but because I already had so much knowledge about the topic I felt that I was not working from a blank slate. Phenomenology was slightly different from grounded theory because my understanding was that if you were using grounded theory you would have absolutely a 'blank slate'.

Lara continues on to explain what she means by the term 'blank slate':

> With grounded theory you would probably not look at any literature, and you would be coding as you are sampling and analysing your data, and then maybe you do some more sampling and so on, depending on what you need. However, I had been through a year's worth of ethics to get my research started so I had

to know how many times I would be speaking to people and who they were. I could not be flexible about recruiting more people and also I had looked at the literature and I did have previous experience, so I felt that I couldn't be a blank slate enough to use grounded theory.

I chose phenomenology as I had already spent a lot of time preparing to do the research so I had some idea of the concepts and themes that related to the topic, so I decided that phenomenology would allow me to use all the preparation as background to my research. The strength in using phenomenology for me was that it appealed to me personally, so I really felt I understood what to do and I liked the fact that it acknowledges that what is discussed is a product of both of the people (the participant and the interviewer) and the way that they are interacting and the way that they are thinking. Also it allows you to have assumptions, providing you acknowledge those and the reader can see where they may have had a role to play in your interpretation, rather than saying, 'I'm completely unbiased', which I thought was impossible.

When asked about the weaknesses of this approach, Lara stated:

It's quite an abstract theoretical process and as an inexperienced researcher it was quite difficult not to get really caught up in 'what is phenomenology?' I had to stop myself from writing a thesis about phenomenology; instead, just use the methodology. I spent a lot of time reading about phenomenology. I was terrified about being criticised and about not being able to justify my approach. I felt like I had to know everything about phenomenology – where it came from, all the different schools of thought, how each one would use it slightly differently. So I would put in big chunks of time where I'm just reading about phenomenology. I realised that you had to know as much about your research methodology as the content of the questions you were trying to answer. I think it's quite complex and very abstract and pretty tricky to get your head around.

WHAT RESEARCH METHODS CAN I CHOOSE?

Some of the most commonly used research methods in qualitative research studies are observations and interviews. These methods are often well understood by those working with young children as they are the same techniques used by them in their professional roles. For example, early childhood teachers would use observations and discussions with children to design learning activities for these children in their early childhood education and care environments. The use of documents is another data source that complements the methods of observation and interviewing. In this section we focus on observations, interviews, field notes and the use of documents. However, in this book there is discussion of other methods that are also relevant to qualitative research, such as narratives, focus groups and visual ethnographic methods, to name just a few.

Observation

Broadly defined, observation is something that we all do as we collect data. However, there are variations of observation techniques, for example naturalistic observation (observing in the participant's daily environment), formal observation (a more systematic process of observing and recording, which can be under 'test' conditions) and participant observation (where the observer is a member of the setting or group under study).

Naturalistic observation is a refining of our observational skills to focus on particular research interests where there is a reliance on our personal data collection rather than using measuring tools. Participant observation provides direct experiential and observational access to the insiders' world of meaning. Participant observation can provide deeper insights into what is occurring. While other research methods 'are limited to reporting about what people say they do' (Gans, 1999, p. 540), the researcher is not only able to see what is happening but also to 'feel what it was like to be part of the group' (Genzuk, 2003, p. 3). In these circumstances it is important that researchers stay focused on their role as 'information gatherer' (Merriam, 1998, p. 101), and remember to record their own 'location' when mapping practices and discourse through their witness accounts (Ropers-Huilman, 1999, p. 29). Participant observation typically generates field notes (described later in this chapter) to record researcher's reflections. Participant observation, and the richness of the descriptions contained in the field notes, contributes to the interpretation, analysis, reliability and verification of the research.

In using observation methods it is important to consider time, duration and frequency of the observations, as well as the procedures used to record them, such as schedules, formats or frameworks for observing.

Interviews

Interviews are commonly used to gather data in qualitative research. The interview process is a valuable data collection tool because usually participants are comfortable with the interview as a communicative event (Miller & Crabtree, 2004; Silverman, 2003). However, establishing a good rapport with participants in an interview is essential (Gerson & Horowitz, 2002; Legard, Keegan & Ward, 2003), and doing so establishes a relationship of trust, respect and credibility. There are several forms of interviews, each of which draws out data in different ways. Some have a formal structure and others are less structured. No matter what the format there are certain protocols that must be followed, such as obtaining informed consent from participants and thinking through how the participant's identity will be protected (see the discussion on ethics in Chapter 6).

Conversational interviews, which are directed by the participants, are effective in methodologies such as phenomenology as they capture feelings, thoughts and experiences in participants' own words (Taylor, 2005). Semi-structured interviews can be conversational as they allow researchers to create a feeling of natural involvement, an interaction between two people (McQueen & Knussen, 2006). As well as asking simple questions, difficult and sensitive questions can be asked in an attempt to elicit responses that focus on the breadth of the participant's experiences. The knowledge generated in the semi-structured interview is about the individual's perspective. The semi-structured interview is a 'partnership on a conversational journey' (Miller & Crabtree, 2004, p. 187) and usually begins as a hierarchical relationship as the interviewer sets the scene, asks the initial questions and follows the traditional rules of an interview. However, as the interview progresses, participants work to develop a relationship and construct meaning together, and so the hierarchy may shift and the rules may change (Holstein & Gubrium, 2003; Legard et al., 2003; Mason, 2002a; Miller & Crabtree, 2004). Figure 7.1 illustrates the steps in the interview process as proposed by Miller and Crabtree (2004, p. 199).

Figure 7.1   Steps in the interview process (Miller & Crabtree, 2004, p. 199), as configured by Cartmel (2007)

As Figure 7.1 shows, the interview begins with some rapport-building biographical questions, with this initial stage involving three steps. The first step of *naturalising* is when the researcher becomes familiar with the setting. The second step, *assigning competence*, occurs when the interviewer and the participant provide biographical details that set the later conversation in context. The third step, *activating the narrative*, occurs when both the interviewer and participant begin to talk about the context of the research theme (Miller & Crabtree, 2004). *Getting the details* and *getting deep* are the middle steps of the interview in order to gather the required data. To ensure that the data are trustworthy and reflect the perspectives of the stakeholders, material is constantly checked during the interview conversation, particularly to ensure that research values have not been imposed through asking leading questions or making subtle misinterpretations (Thomas, 1993). The final interview steps are *toning down* and *closing*. In these steps the interviewer ensures that the interviewee is feeling comfortable with the material they have described and discussed during the interview. The interviewer confirms with the interviewee how the data is going to be used within the research project.

Researchers ask questions that pertain to the area of interest, and ones that probe beyond the surface. Flexibility in asking probing questions is important so that issues or themes can be pursued to gather 'thick descriptions' (Geertz, 1973). The interviews are not controlled verbal exchanges because in each interview there are multiple layers of messages being conveyed. Collecting verbal data means that the content can be clarified immediately, which assists with data validation (Lawson, 1985).

As previously mentioned, Lara had decided to use phenomenology as the methodology for her research design. She then had to decide on the tools that would best allow her to collect her data. In this case, mainly interviews were used.

To me the best option was to conduct one-on-one interviews with my participants and use field notes as my data collection methods. I used a reflective journal and looked at what my own presuppositions might be and tried to acknowledge where they came through my analysis in my interpretations. For example, in my journal and then in my thesis, I acknowledged that, 'I noticed that this person was nervous so maybe that influenced my analysis on that day'. I basically made sure that I had an ordered trail, as much as I could, for the actual decision-making processes in the analysis and that was slightly different from grounded theory.

When asked about advice she would give to others contemplating using interviewing as a data collection method, Lara offered the following:

> It is important to have a rough topic guide, a framework of questions. However, it is just as important to make the interview more like a conversation, with the participant leading the conversation and me asking probing questions so that together we could examine what they were thinking. Even though I had a framework of questions, it was not necessary to ask them all, or in any order, and if someone were to bring something up, it was important to explore that. As a qualitative methodology, it was theory-generating and inductive, not testing anything.

Tackling transcribing interview data

The act of transcribing is a selective process. Therefore, you need to tailor the transcription so that it is useful to the research being undertaken. No matter how well the interview data is recorded, there is some data loss during transcription due to the fact that the non-verbal aspects of the situation cannot be captured in text and the transcript therefore becomes decontextualised. This means that during an interview the researcher must take care to note the tone and inflection in the speaker's voice, the silences that occur, where emphasis is placed, the speed of delivery, the continuity of the speech, the speaker's mood, and any other non-verbal behaviour as it occurs (Cohen, Manion, & Morrison, 2011). There are differing views as to who should transcribe the data. There are those researchers who uphold the view that it should be the researchers themselves who transcribe the data as a way to encourage a more immersed level of engagement with the data. Other researchers, however, do not see the need for this and engage a transcriber, who types the transcripts verbatim. Whichever way you work, you will need to revisit the recorded versions many times to really capture the aspects that a verbatim transcription alone cannot capture.

Field notes

Field notes are a long-established method of data collection and are particularly useful in ethnographic research (Arthur & Nazroo, 2003). They are used to capture primary data from observations, and in interviews to complement issues for consideration, such as the context of an interview. The field notes contain information about negotiating access, entry and rapport during the data collection process, and are useful for describing researcher relations (Harrington, 2003). The notes written about the research circumstances can be 'evocative' and capture complexities that are not available from interview or direct observation (Emerson, 2001, p. 134). Field notes are also a valuable tool in the validation process. Researcher reflection, introspection and self-monitoring expose all the phases of the research to continual questioning and re-evaluation (Emerson, 2001; Lofland & Lofland, 1995; Merriam, 2002). The notes should contain information about time, place and purpose. There is no right way or correct format for field notes, but they must contain much detail to provide thick descriptions of the data. In recording field notes, it is important to ensure that the terms used in descriptions have consistent meanings. Emerson, Fretz, and Shaw (1995) recommend that enhanced awareness of writing field notes encourages researchers, particularly ethnographers, to be more attentive to details while in the field.

Documents

Documents as sources of data refer to a range of written, visual and physical material pertinent to the research project. Sometimes using documents can verify, contextualise or clarify the data collected from interviews and observations (Mason, 2002b). The ethical issues that relate to the observation and interviewing process also apply to the use of the documents. Some documents can be private or confidential in form and it can be difficult to establish informed consent (Mason, 2002b). The owners or the keepers of the documents are not able, in every case, to give permission to use the document because it implicates other people. The role of the researcher is not to criticise or assess the texts, but rather to 'analyse how they work to achieve particular effects' (Silverman, 2003, p. 152). Documents as data are particularly useful when the history of circumstances have relevance (Ritchie & Lewis, 2003).

HOW ARE RELIABILITY AND VALIDITY ENSURED WHEN TAKING A QUALITATIVE APPROACH TO RESEARCH?

For qualitative research, attention to the design, implementation and analysis needs to be focused. Trustworthiness of the process is required, and this is driven by integrity and meticulous and ethical practice. For some forms of practitioner inquiry, validity is measured by the trustworthiness of the study (Mishler, 1990), or the quality, authority and grounding of autobiographical research (Bullough & Pinnegar, 2001). Alternative criteria for valuing practitioner research, as suggested by Cochran-Smith and Donnell (2006, p. 510), comprise of five aspects of validity: democratic validity (honouring the perspectives and interests of all stakeholders), outcome validity (resolving the problem addressed), process validity (using appropriate and adequate research methods and inquiry processes), catalytic validity (deepening the understandings of all the participants), and dialogic validity (monitoring analysis through critical and reflective discussion with peers).

Some researchers suggest that for qualitative research, the focus should turn from validity and reliability to dependability and the consistency of the findings from the data analyses (Lincoln & Guba, 1985). This is achievable by being explicit about the whole research process. Guba (1981) determines the criteria for validity of qualitative research as credibility (that all complexities of the study have been taken into account, including the ability to deal with patterns that are not easily explained), transferability (the context-bound nature of the research), dependability (data stability), and confirmability (the objectivity of the data). Some suggestions offered to meet these criteria include collecting data over a longer time frame, using triangulation, collecting detailed descriptive data, overlapping methods, establishing an 'audit trail', and being reflexive. For example, to achieve construct validity when undertaking a case study, you would need to develop a sufficiently operational set of measures to collect your data, and clearly outline the chain of evidence that links things together. Wolcott (1994) offers the following strategies for ensuring the validity of action research: talk little; listen a lot; record accurately; begin writing early; let readers 'see' for themselves; report fully; be candid; seek feedback; and write accurately. Internal validity can be guaranteed by building into your research design aspects such as triangulation, rechecking with participants as to researcher interpretations, peer judgement, and long-term observation. MacNaughton and Hughes (2009) regard triangulation as being categorised into four types:

- triangulation of data (involving the use of diverse data sources about the topic);
- triangulation of methods (employing multiple methods to study the topic);
- triangulation of investigators (using more than one researcher to study the topic); and
- triangulation of theory (applying multiple theories to interpret the same data set about the topic).

For qualitative studies, internal validity refers to the 'extent to which the findings faithfully represent and reflect the reality that has been studied' (Punch, 2009, p. 315). First, establish internal consistency (all parts of the research should fit together and findings should have internal consistency and coherence). Second, make the ways in which conclusions have been drawn and confirmed explicit and logical. For example, consider negative evidence, cross-validate findings and eliminate rival hypotheses. Qualitative research can also use 'member checking' where the researcher checks their interpretations of data with participants. The way the study has been designed and conducted, along with the presentation and analysis of the evidence, combine to assess the strength of the internal validity of a study. An excerpt from Andrea's doctoral thesis, a qualitative research study which aimed to investigate the history of early childhood teacher training in Victoria, Australia, in order to identify the critical factors influencing dominant views of knowledge, describes how she worked to ensure that her data was valid and accurate.

> One important reason for organising data into some type of system as early as possible was so that the shortcoming of data overload did not occur. This can lead to important information being overlooked, skewing the analysis or adding too much weight to some findings, which can have an effect on the verification process. From my earliest days in the field I began checking and cross-checking what I had been hearing and reading. I would pose some of my tentative interpretations as questions in interview situations just to have them confirmed or denied. My conclusions were also tested by checking for representativeness, checking for researcher effects (reactivity), as well as triangulation and weighing the evidence. It was the feedback I received from participants which helped verify conclusions – validation by the respondents. By the process of searching for disconfirming evidence validity was strengthened.

As can be seen from this excerpt, checking and double-checking results from multiple sources helps to build the validity process into the data collection (Miles & Huberman, 1994). An example of how this could work when interviewing young children would be to conduct more than one interview (Rasmusson, 2011). Searching for conflicting as well as complementary accounts has also been used with much success. In fact, it is the competence, skill, thoroughness, rigour, control and care of the researcher that determines the validity of qualitative research. Another example comes from Lara, who was very conscious about building a process to ensure her study's findings were reliable and valid. As Lara's study involved interviewing 53 participants, the large amount of data generated created pressure on her in relation to not only transcribing but also analysing the data. She developed and subsequently explained in detail in the 'Findings' and 'Discussion' chapters of her thesis, the process she developed whereby she would explicitly make connections between previous interviews and current interviews. As she explained, it had to be obvious to those outside the study how this came together so that her study would 'stand up' to scrutiny.

WHAT DO I NEED TO CONSIDER WHEN THINKING ABOUT QUALITATIVE DATA ANALYSIS?

Decisions relating to data analysis need to be determined early on in the research design stage and informed by the theoretical perspective which has underpinned your research (Mukherji & Albon, 2010). Your beliefs about the nature of research will determine the way the analysis proceeds and what is privileged in the analysis. The consequence is that your data collection methods determine the type of data collected and this in turn determines the choice of data analysis. Ask yourself: 'Have I collected data that is more qualitative in nature or data that is more quantitative in nature, or is my data a mixture of both?' If your data is numerical in nature you will take a more quantitative approach and apply statistical analysis (see Chapter 8), whereas if your data is more qualitative in nature, then you will be choosing data analysis methods that can identify patterns and themes within the data.

You may have qualitative data which is in a written form, encompassing surveys, observations, field notes, questionnaires, tests, assessments, computer text files, diaries or narratives. Audio recordings may have been utilised, such as digital voice recordings of observations, interviews, focus group discussions, singing, music or field recordings. Data may also consist of visual records, such as work samples, drawings, concept or mind-maps, paintings, designs, photographs or video footage. Having a variety of different data sources is not an issue if managed in a systematic way. The data analysis method(s) should be able to assist you to look across the data sets to begin to make sense of what you may have found. For example, you may be able to cluster together key issues or themes in preparation for drawing conclusions, being mindful of including all data that proves your 'hunches' or hypotheses as well as the data that may present an alternative view. It is important that you start your data analysis with no preconceptions about what you will find, being open to having your ideas challenged and allowing for alternative explanations to emerge.

When working from a qualitative perspective, the categorisation of data is often an intuitive process, as you become more familiar with the data, but it is informed by the research questions and research design. You will need to read and reread your transcripts, revisit your audio/video data, consistently sorting, reviewing and reflecting on the data you have collected to assist you to identify patterns, regularities or aspects of interest which can be highlighted as potential categories around which to align your themes. This can happen while the data collection is still in progress and is a common practice in qualitative research projects. Bell (2010) suggests that it is best to start with some broad categories rather than having many categories only to find that some are not substantiated. For those researchers involved in naturalistic and ethnographic research, this is a painstaking process as it calls for the meticulous taking apart of field notes, comparing, contrasting, aggregating, sifting, sorting and ordering notes, with the intention of moving from rich description to explanation and the generation of theory (Cohen et al., 2011).

If you are taking a qualitative approach using interview data, your analysis will be interpretive, presenting as a 'reflexive, reactive interaction between the researcher and the decontextualized data that are already interpretations of a social encounter' (Cohen et al., 2011, p. 427) and should be presented in this light. One researcher, Christine, writes about the dilemma which confronted her as she began interpreting interview data taking a qualitative approach:

> In the case of the interviews, interpreting the voice of others led to the development of yet another voice... a different voice. My dilemma as a researcher was to critically reconstruct and re-present the voices of the participants in a way that took account of their humanity, integrity and struggle (Britzman, 1991). I was aware of the importance of taking the necessary stances of a listener: methodological humility and methodological caution (Narayan, 1988). Applying these stances, I was encouraged not to see accounts as full representations of the context and to ensure that the critiquing of these accounts did not act to denigrate, dismiss or detract from the view of the participant. To be true to this way of working I developed tentative perspectives related to contexts and then checked these by directly asking participants about their applicability to a particular situation. Verified perspectives were then considered to be part of the total set of perspectives. This enabled me to undertake analysis work while I was still out in the field collecting data.

When analysing observations, you need to ensure that the behaviour to be analysed is understood in the same manner by all observers. Uniformity in behavioural interpretation is critical to the accuracy and integrity of your data. Checking your analysis with the participant is also a way of ensuring you are making the correct judgements. The following example is taken from the Young Learners Project, which aimed to identify factors in a 4-year-old preschooler's educational program, home-life or personal characteristics that were positively associated with the development of strong literacy outcomes in their first year of school education. In this project, early childhood teachers were videoed taking three literacy experiences – one relating to reading, one relating to writing and the other a literacy experience of their choice. The video data was then analysed by the research team. To enable the early childhood teachers themselves to support or challenge the researchers' interpretations of their practice, an opportunity was provided where the researchers met with each educator and together they viewed excerpts of the video data and discussed the practice. This allowed for a deeper level of analysis to occur, one which involved the participant in the process, while also adding to the validity of the interpretations on the part of the researchers.

If choosing to use a software package to assist with data analysis, you need to allow time to fully investigate the strengths and weakness of available software and whether the package will enable you to process the data in the manner you intend. Popular software programs include Leximancer and NVivo. Leximancer allows you to examine concepts, not just key words, of the textual data that has been gathered. NVivo software supports qualitative and mixed methods research by allowing you to search, query and use visualisation tools. These programs provide an automated and time-effective way of analysing qualitative data. However, some researchers are wary of using software, feeling that they are not in control of the analysis, whereas others enjoy the experience of applying a software program, which allows them to analyse the data from a variety of angles depending on the way the process is applied. It is crucial when employing any type of data analysis software that you have a good understanding of the process being applied, the appropriate way to set up data within the software package, and the correct method to perform the desired analysis.

It is critical to stay focused on your research question(s) when analysing your data. During your research journey many interesting aspects may arise that have the potential to distract your attention from the true intention of your research project. It is during the analysis stage that you must keep the intent of your research in the forefront of your mind and continually ask yourself: Does this answer my question or questions? Baumfield, Hall, and Wall (2008) suggest that you keep a diary of all the questions you ask of the data in an analysis log. While initially this may appear time-consuming, it circumvents later reanalysis as you can check back through your records to see if you have already looked at the data in a certain way, asking a particular question of it.

When involved in any analysis of data you must also be alert to the following:

- representing the data without misrepresenting the meaning;
- being objective rather than subjective in your interpretations of the data;
- not allowing your judgment to be influenced by previous knowledge you may have about the subject or event;
- using appropriate methods;
- identifying other factors that could be impacting on the results;

- making appropriate, sustainable and well supported inferences, generalisations and/or recommendations according to the data;
- avoiding the selective and unrepresentative use of data.

(Cohen et al., 2011, pp. 116–117)

What you will quickly realise is that any decisions you make during the data collection period (which sites, which participants, which data collection approaches), as well as the manipulation of the data you will be involved in along the way (constructing summaries, coding, allocating themes, clustering), will all impact on the final findings of the study. The choices made can be considered as 'analytic choices' and thereby become part of the analysis process (Miles & Huberman, 1994, p. 21). We now return to Lara's story and the large data set generated from her phenomenological inquiry. As you read through the following excerpt from a conversation with her about her data analysis, you will see some of the analysis processes, discussed in this section, that need to be considered.

> My method of analysis was a form of interpretive phenomenological analysis so that basically was a process of coding, looking for themes and patterns and examining meanings in the transcripts in order to develop a set of themes. Then I discussed the relationships between those themes, and then moved to a more abstract level of how the themes were interconnecting over the whole data set. Finally, I developed a conceptual model of explaining the relationships between them.

HOW DO I ORGANISE THE DATA INTO A USABLE FORM TO AID DATA ANALYSIS?

In order for data to have meaning it needs to be recorded in such a way that it can be interpreted and analysed. It is therefore essential to have a plan that is logical and relates directly to the research question(s). There are a number of ways to organise your information. For example, you may choose to present similarities or differences found across the data, patterns that begin to be identified, significant issues or events as they become apparent, or use predetermined categories taken from the literature or previous research.

Perhaps the simplest way to begin is by developing a table which lists all the data sources you have collected, the number of participants in each sample, and the associated time frames over which data collection occurred. This will give you an overview of your data collection. You can then reflect on how well each method worked. For example, did it measure what you expected it to? These reflections will help you consider the validity and reliability of the data and help you 'prioritise your thinking about the different sets of results' (Baumfield, Hall, & Wall, 2008, p. 102).

The process of organising your data should not wait until you have completed your data collection; rather it should be a continuous process throughout the study. For instance, if you have interviewed participants, you will need to transcribe the interviews so the responses are in a usable form ready for coding. This also applies to surveys and questionnaires. If you have used a survey, consider in what format the answers are given. You can then make decisions about the best ways to present these responses. This process is known as data reduction. Transferring all respondents responses on to a spreadsheet may be a good starting point as this will allow you to see all answers from each participant to each question at a glance, or you may like to try assigning codes to each response, where possible. This database will then be ready for further analysis, first checking the data for completeness, accuracy and uniformity.

By organising data as it is collected, or at designated points within the research journey, you are able to act in a responsive, reflective and informed way. This process streamlines your data collection by identifying significant and non-significant aspects which helps to further refine your methods during the process.

To determine interesting findings you may consider recording the data on index cards, or constructing graphs, tables, diagrams and pie charts. These will assist you to make sense of the data. When looking at the data in a visual manner, you can ask yourself if any of the findings warrant further investigation, or if anything appears significant or significantly different, or if there are recurring patterns present. Data can be organised around the theoretical proposition on which the study is based or, if that is not relevant, a more descriptive framework of events can also help you to organise your data ready for more detailed analysis.

HOW DO I CODE DATA?

Coding data is a method often applied to qualitative data. Coding enables the researcher to allocate meaning to the data. When you assign a code to a piece of data you are signalling units of meaning. The coding process helps uncover similarities within the data, thus enabling the data to be clustered together. This provides an organising structure that can be aligned to research questions or themes.

What is coded will be determined by the study design, as individual words, sentences or paragraphs can become part of a code. The following example, taken from a study entitled 'Exploring and evaluating levels of reflection in pre-service early childhood teachers' (Nolan & Sim, 2011), illustrates the coding process undertaken by two experienced researchers.

The data collected for this research project comprised pre-service teachers' written responses to guided reflection tasks as part of an early childhood teacher training course. To analyse the data, Henri's thematic unit of analysis (Herrington & Oliver, 1999) was adopted due to its flexibility in coding data. Henri's thematic unit refers to counting each 'unit of meaning' by extracting the meaning from the text without the constraint of word, sentence or paragraph limitation (Herrington & Oliver, 1999). Therefore, the length of the unit of meaning is dependent on the writing style of the participants, in this case pre-service early childhood teachers, allowing for flexibility when coding. As the data involved participants' learning and reflections, explicit statements were the norm and subtle meanings were a rarity. Thus the issues of increased subjectivity and low coding reliability associated with coding for more subtle themes posed less of a problem in this study (Rourke, Anderson, Garrison, & Archer, 2001).

Coding can take place early on in the study during the development of the data collection tools. Surveys and interview questions can be allocated a code which enables responses to be instantly aligned with a particular code as soon as they are collected. The following guidelines can be considered when assigning codes either pre- or post-data collection: (1) codes must be mutually exclusive; (2) categories should be exhaustive; (3) codes must be applied consistently (Mukherji & Albon, 2010). Coded responses can be easily organised into related groups, chunks or themes. Lara provides a very honest description of the coding processes which she undertook with her data:

> I went through a very long process. I did all the transcription myself. I would say it comes with a warning, though, because that is the most monotonous task of the whole thing, and then leading straight into coding as well – that was for me the black hole. I transcribed and then I used NVivo 2 data management software. Then I coded in very fine detail every interview one by one. I didn't start with any themes. I basically started off coding down to word, phrase, sentence level with each interview and basically generating a load of free nodes. Then throughout the whole process I started to collect nodes like 4 into 1, and 5 into 1, and so on and so on. NVivo also allows you to save every single version so it takes up masses of hard disc space, but if I wanted to go back and say 'Well, what did I have before I put that thing in?' or 'Where was my thinking on just the second transcript?' I could do that. I generated masses of codes and I had to spend weeks refining and merging these. So yes, I did consolidate the initial coding, recoding it with new convoluted codes to see whether they were really a theme. I looked at each code to see if they could pick up every single excerpt and then I started to interrogate the codes. So grouping the codes into sets by research question would be one example, or a candidate theme, and then do those reports again and then you can compare codes to other codes and see whether they are co-occurring. Then I started to play around with candidate

themes (emerging potential proposed themes not at a stage of refinement) and take them back on to the data and look at whether there was evidence – so if I was going to write about that theme now, what sort of evidence would I be able to draw on across the whole data set?

For some themes I got to the point where I had a framework or a hierarchy of themes and sub-themes, and at that stage I started taking those back and really making sure that there was evidence to support them, that they were substantiated. I set rough levels in my mind and a minimum number of participants that a theme had to relate to, otherwise it was not considered. I worked up close and also distant from the data at different points, but at that stage where I had the themes, I moved away and I experimented with different ways of grouping the themes. I tried to move to a more abstract level of explanation, so rather than just having themes which said something about a pattern in the data, I was trying to get to more of an explanatory level. For example, one of the themes was 'Practitioners' ideas or accounts of how symbols should be used' and so above that came their professional reasoning. That was the more abstract level of it – the conceptual model level.

Lara's account of the process she followed regarding her analysis provides a very detailed view of the complexities and second-guessing you can experience once you begin analysing your qualitative data.

WHAT ARE THE DIFFERENT APPROACHES TO ANALYSING QUALITATIVE DATA?

Qualitative approaches of data analysis include discourse analysis, narrative analysis, conversation analysis, grounded theory, and content analysis. These approaches are briefly outlined below. However, to gain a more in-depth understanding it is best to consult texts that focus on the analysis approach you choose.

Discourse analysis

Discourse analysis is the in-depth, critical analysis of the social relations within data 'texts' (spoken or written). It deconstructs and interprets texts and can be seen as a way of thinking about issues with a view to accessing the ontological and epistemological assumptions within such texts. It focuses on the use of language and how it produces and reproduces notions of what constitutes appropriate ways of being. If, taking a Foucauldian approach, texts are examined to see how the power of dominant discourses play out in the language of the texts (Cohen et al., 2011), this means that the researcher explores the dominance of particular discourses which prioritise certain ways of acting or thinking. These ways of acting and thinking are legitimated by the more powerful voices within societies. This methodology is action-based as it acts to construct meaning in the social contexts in which the 'text' is created. It therefore requires 'a careful reading and interpretation of textual material, with interpretation being supported by the linguistic evidence' (Cohen et al., 2011, p. 451). We suggest that this is taken in stages, with the first stage being the assigning of codes to determine themes and patterns within the discourse, followed by a closer examination of the text 'to discover intensions, functions and consequences of the discourse (examining the speech act functions of the discourse, i.e. to impart information, to persuade, to accuse, to censure, to encourage, etc.)' (Cohen et al., 2011, p. 451). By looking for 'alternative explanations and the degree of variability in the discourse', other interpretations can be eliminated, leading to a 'fair reading of what was actually taking place in the discourse in its social context' (Cohen et al., 2011, p. 451). When working with texts using discourse analysis you will need to be mindful that 'any interpretations will always be through our own sociocultural and historical lens' (Mukherji & Albon, 2010, p. 156). You will need to be highly reflective as you will also be creating a discourse through your analysis.

Narrative analysis

Narrative analysis does not attempt to code the data but rather considers each 'story' as a whole. This type of analysis takes into consideration the content, form and context of the emerging story. 'The skills involved are to summarise and interpret the data while retaining the participants' voices and views' (O'Hara, Carter, Dewis, Kay, & Wainwright, 2011, p. 215). Cohen et al. (2011) suggest that once the researcher uncovers the characteristics of the narrative, such as the inclusion of critical moments, complicating factors, evaluation and outcomes, decisions can be made in relation to his or her own research question. The researcher can then analyse and interpret the text for the meanings contained in it, develop working hypotheses to explain what is taking place, check these hypotheses against the data and the remainder of the text, see the text as a whole rather than as discrete units, and ensure that different interpretations of the text have been considered and the one(s) chosen are the most secure in terms of fidelity to the text (Cohen et al., 2011, p. 553).

The focus of narrative analysis is on how the participants make and use stories, viewing them as social products shaped by social, cultural and historical contexts. Researchers search for the threads in each story that link to the storied landscape temporality, sociality and place. These are then analysed using a theoretical perspective (Clandinin, 2006). The last stage in the analysis process is the construction of the final narrative. 'Narrative analysis, together with biographical data, can give the added dimension of realism, authenticity, humanity, personality, emotions, views and values in a situation, and the research must ensure that these are featured in the narratives that have been constructed' (Cohen et al., 2011, p. 553). Narrative analysis works to keep the text and content together to produce a united whole.

Conversation analysis

Conversation analysis focuses on the spoken discourse and involves a fine grain analysis of speech episodes. As MacLure and Walker (2007) explain, 'it is concerned with the ways in which speakers produce order, meaning and coherence in and through their interactions' (p. 221). This method of analysis is driven by the data which captures naturally occurring interactions focusing on what the speakers are doing and demonstrating as relevant in their talk. It focuses on the features of the conversation, its construction and operation, distinguishing features, and how meaning is constructed within the conversation (Cohen et al., 2011). Conversation analysis is not a method that labels actions in interactions; instead the focus is on uncovering the co-construction of the actions and what is being privileged, or orientated to, within these interactions, thereby providing multi-levelled interpretations of conversations as discourses (Sacks, 1984). The process sees the weaving of analysis and interpretation, which raises issues of validity and reliability, like most qualitative approaches. Conversation analysis is considered an ideal method of investigating interaction involving young children (Danby, 2002).

Grounded theory

The grounded theory approach generates theory from the data rather than the data from theory; theory is therefore positioned as emergent. 'It is a process of inductive theory building based squarely on observation of the data themselves' (Crotty, 1998, p. 78). It is systematic in approach and involves common practices such as theoretical sampling, coding, constant comparison, the core variable(s) and 'saturation' (Cohen et al., 2011). These are explained as the continuation of data collection until enough data is at hand to fully understand what is occurring, disassembling and reassembling the data to create new understandings, comparing new data with existing data, the identification of a core variable through the process of comparison, and the exhaustion of any new insights (Cohen et al., 2011). O'Hara et al. (2011) outline three stages to grounded theory analysis relating to coding:

1 Open coding, in which the raw data is coded according to conceptual categories that the researcher finds within the data through the process of 'identifying a range of indicators and comparing them' (p. 214).
2 Axial coding, in which connections are made between the initial conceptual categories.
3 Selective coding, in which 'the researcher determines a central category drawn from the analysis thus far and this becomes the theoretical aspect of the research' (p. 241).

Working in this way, the inquiry is seen, 'through a series of carefully planned steps, [to] develop theoretical ideas' (Crotty, 1998, p. 78).

Content analysis

The purpose of using the content analysis method is to compress larger amounts of text into fewer categories by applying rules to guide the coding and generate 'replicable and valid inferences from the data to their context' (Krippendorff, 1980, p. 21). Content analysis is about looking at how words or concepts are used in the data and taking note of the frequency of their use and meaning. Its focus is on what is said rather than why it is said, and follows a systematic and rigorous process to ensure it is representing the contents of the data. The defining of the 'unit' that will be the focus of study needs to be carefully determined before implementing this form of analysis and the sampling procedure chosen needs to be followed for all data sources. As Burns (2000) warns, 'content analysis needs a coding system that relates to the theoretical framework or research question' (p. 434). Brenner, Brown, and Canter (1985) propose the following steps to inform the analysis process with open-ended data:

- briefing – understanding the problem and context;
- sampling – who is included;
- associating – drawing links with other similar work;
- hypothesis development;
- hypothesis testing;
- immersion – becoming familiar with the data;
- categorising – creating exhaustive and mutually exclusive categories from the data;
- incubation – reflecting on the data and interpretations;
- synthesis – reviewing rationale for coding and identifying emerging patterns and themes;
- culling – discarding and condensing data so it can be reported in an intelligible way;

- interpretation – drawing meaning from the data;
- writing – making things clear to the reader; and
- rethinking (cited in Cohen et al., 2011, p. 428).

Content analysis has the capacity to be used with both qualitative and quantitative data, as it has the capability to count and code data rather than uncover a deeper level of meaning within the analysis. In using this approach to data analysis, the researcher is able to control the independent variable – for what they choose to search and over what time period, and in which places.

Lara offers the following advice to beginning researchers:

> I think novice researchers interested in taking a qualitative approach should read some of the general guides to qualitative research, particularly when they have an approach in mind. Do some reading but don't expect there to be any clear step-by-step guides because there isn't and that's something that you spend the whole time looking for. I think 'journal' everything. Record every decision. But don't question yourself too much. You are going to have a subjective thought process in this whole thing, that's the way it works. But you need to find a way to express it to another person. And if something is not working, say you've generated 6000 codes, then don't be afraid to say 'I'm going to start that again' and recode because again you are still absorbing the meaning.

WHAT DO I NEED TO BE MINDFUL OF IF I WANT CHILDREN TO BE MORE INVOLVED IN THE RESEARCH PROCESS?

The way we attend to a situation, individually and collectively, will determine how successful we are in providing the best environments in which children can become active agents in their own lives. This success depends on the ability not only to talk and listen to the views of children, but to engage them in the research process itself. When conducting research involving children, you will need to be alert to how you position children, which will determine the research design. Thought has to go into what the adult role will be, as well as the methods of data collection employed. Tisdall, Davis, and Gallagher (2009) propose that rather than make a distinction between appropriate methods to use with adults and those to use with children, thinking should focus more on 'the particular children you are engaging with – the communication forms they like to use, the contexts in which they are, their own characteristics' (p. 7).

Kinney (2006) proposes that conversations with children are as important as conversations with adults and that there is an obligation to truly listen to children. This sentiment is echoed in the United Nations Convention on the Rights of the Child, Article 12, which declares that children have the right to be heard. To listen to children, Macfarlane, Cartmel, and Nolan (2011) suggest that having a mindful presence; observing, reflecting and applying a strong sense of justice (Macfarlane & Cartmel, 2008) are useful strategies to employ. This sentiment of being committed to actively listening, being respectful and engaging in a dialectic process is supported by other researchers (Dockett & Perry, 2011).

In order for children to feel uninhibited by an adult's natural authority or perceived power, the analysis process must be comprised of open and ongoing dialogue with the children. Mackey and Vaealiki (2011) dealt with this issue by employing a number of strategies, such as waiting for the children to invite them into their play, engaging in conversations with the children rather than asking questions, and joining in the normal routines that occurred in the setting in an attempt to make data gathering as unobtrusive and natural as possible. Amber, the undergraduate student whose study involved the use of mind-maps with children as a data collection tool (introduced in Chapter 6), involved the children in authenticating her interpretation of the data by having respectful dialogue with the children about the mind-maps she collaboratively created with them.

When children are involved in research you will need to consider what form this involvement will take. Will the children be providing feedback regarding your findings in an ongoing way in order for you to check the authenticity or your understandings, or will children be involved in other ways? Gallagher (2009) suggests that children, where and when appropriate, should be given a choice on how the data should be recorded and be active agents in the recording process. For example, a researcher may hand control of the taping device to the child, or allow them to use the interview schedule to interview each other. Other methods of involving children in the data collection process include providing children with digital cameras, or recording devices and allowing them to decide what they wish to record. Allowing children to take researchers on a tour of their setting has also been proven as an effective way for children to communicate their perspectives and point out things they feel are important (Clark & Moss, 2001; Mackey & Vaealiki, 2011). If you want to share the data with the children, you will need to record it in a way that makes it accessible for them. Discussing your understandings or presenting the findings pictorially are ways that assist young children to engage with the data. Presenting data to children takes time and planning.

Deciding where and when children will be involved in the research process needs to be made clear in the initial design of your research project, noting that 'in practice children's roles within projects can be variable due to lack of time, confidence, interest or skills' (Davis, 2009, p. 164). However, this does not mean that it is not worth investigating ways to enable young children to participate in a number of roles in the research process.

REFLECTION POINTS

When thinking about applying qualitative methodologies in your research, consider the following questions:

- What methodologies do I feel most attracted to and why?
- How will the chosen methodology allow me to answer my research question(s)?
- What do I need to consider regarding the validity and reliability of my study?
- What options do I have for data collection methods for my study?
- Which methods do I feel most comfortable using and why?
- What time, availability and commitment can I ask for or expect from the study participants?
- What is the timeline I have available to collect data?

Let your data analysis be guided by the following questions (taken from Gallagher, 2009, pp. 83 & 86):

- Do you have a theory or hypothesis that you want to test or refine, or do you want to begin with the data and see what emerges?
- Do you want to merely describe your object of study, or would you also like to explain or understand what you have observed?
- Do you want to compare your data across different cases or variables?
- Do you want to make generalisable claims that might be representative of larger populations, or are you more interested in making a detailed analysis of a small group of children?
- Do you want to synthesise your data to produce a few simple findings, or are you more interested in illuminating differences and demonstrating complexity?
- Do you want to involve children in the process of analysis? What benefits would this bring? What resources would it require?
- How will you analyse non-textual, non-numerical data in ways that capture their complexity and richness?
- What does giving 'voice' to children mean, if the way we deal with children's voices is to render them into text rather than listening to how they sound?
- What are the implications of this focus on text for analysing the lives of children who do not use language?

☐ Summary

This chapter has focused on methodologies, methods and data analysis when taking a qualitative approach to research. It has introduced some of the qualitative research methodologies that are often used by researchers, particularly those who are interested in children. A focus has been on the importance of:

- determining data analysis decisions early on in the research design stage, which has been informed by the theoretical perspective underpinning the research;
- staying focused on the intent of the research throughout the analysis stage;
- considering how children can be involved in data collection and analysis, and the ramifications of this for the project design and implementation.

8 TAKING THE QUANTITATIVE METHODOLOGICAL TRAIL

This chapter focuses on quantitative methodological pathways, introducing the reader to quantitative research approaches. The chapter discusses how quantitative approaches are relevant for research projects, and takes a few methods and provides some in-depth insight into what type of data they generate. This chapter also focuses on the management and analysis of quantitative data. Some of the different approaches to data analysis are outlined, giving an overview of commonly used statistical procedures. Key terminology is also introduced to help develop a basic understanding, thereby enabling the researcher to read more widely and selectively on the method of analysis most appropriate for a particular research project. The chapter concludes with a section about mixed methods approaches. Also, we read Amy's thoughts about her choice of methodology and methods, we meet Karen, as she discusses issues of validity and reliability related to her study, where she aimed to describe the development of a standardised, norm-referenced assessment in the area of child-initiated play, and Kym shares her research team's approach to *bricolage*, a mixed method approach.

Key chapter questions are:

- Why would I choose to conduct a quantitative research study?
- What research approaches could I choose?
- How are reliability and validity ensured when taking a quantitative approach to research?
- How do I choose a representative sample for my study?
- What do I need to consider when thinking about quantitative data analysis?
- What does taking a mixed methods approach mean?
- How do I go about analysing mixed method data?

WHY WOULD I CHOOSE TO CONDUCT A QUANTITATIVE RESEARCH STUDY?

Broadly speaking, methodologies can be defined as qualitative (see Chapter 7) or quantitative. Some studies are a mixture of both and are known as mixed methods. It is argued that taking a mixed methods approach overcomes biases in other approaches as mixed methods research is not subject to the limitations of either quantitative or qualitative approaches. Each form of methodology has strengths and weaknesses and the researcher needs to decide which form is more applicable to their particular context or research issue, the nature of the research, the theoretical perspective underpinning the research design, and the type of information required. Furthermore, the research methodology needs to reflect the kind of question you are trying to answer, or the hypothesis you are testing. The strength of quantitative methodologies is in 'precision and control. Control is achieved through the sampling and design; precision through quantitative and reliable measurement' (Burns, 2000, p. 9).

Quantitative research generates data that is numerical in nature and which will need to be analysed using statistics. Taking this path usually aligns with a positivist theoretical perspective, where the belief is that a theory or hypothesis needs to be tested to see if it is true or not. This calls for controlled testing, the use of inferential statistics to test the hypothesis, using descriptive statistics, multidimensional measurement and factor analysis, and the interpretation of statistical results. This means that the types of sampling and research design applied need careful consideration.

Amy chose to use quantitative research methods for her research project with children and families. She had many thoughts to share about her choice of methodology and the issues that surrounded recruitment of participants and the time-consuming nature of her chosen data collection method. Her project was actually a mixed methodology research project, although there was a greater focus on the quantitative methods. Amy describes her initial thoughts about choosing the quantitative approach:

> When I did my literature review I found that there were a few qualitative studies but not a lot of quantitative studies with a focus on early childhood and gifted development. There was one large longitudinal quantitative study which I found quite inspiring as it presented some interesting results that I was interested in gaining more information on. I think if you've got a strong quantitative study it's a really solid foundation from which you can build a qualitative study. I think this is particularly relevant in the area of giftedness. Often the definition of giftedness is tied to IQ measures and tied to numbers such as IQ scores. But this is only one way of exploring IQ. In my study, I was using IQ measures but I was also exploring other notions of measuring intelligence.

Amy reports that once she had decided on the quantitative approach, she had to choose data collection methods that would provide her with the appropriate information that would also suit the characteristics of the participants involved in the research:

> I was observing a toddler who was demonstrating very advanced symbolic thinking. However, their IQ was assessed as not so high. It made me question: was the observation of play incorrect or the IQ incorrect? I wanted to challenge the notion of IQ and giftedness and so I decided that I had to use a quantitative methodology.

The use of this approach was not without its challenges, especially in relation to researching with young children, as Amy explained:

> You have all the weaknesses of using those standardised measures associated with IQ. You miss so much information by bringing the data down to a number. In my head, all those rich interactions that toddlers are exhibiting are not really described by a single number. I wanted qualitative data as well.

Embarking on a project that was more quantitative in approach did cause Amy some angst initially. One example of this was when one of the mother's withdrew from the project once she found out that an IQ test for her child was part of the process. So while Amy felt comfortable with the processes she was using, not all the participants felt the same way. However, she became more and more curious of what the quantitative methods and data might generate:

> Some people told me that because I was only an early childhood teacher working with young children that I would not be able to do it. Also, I was concerned about the statistics. It wasn't an issue until I came to data analysis and then I did have some assistance. In some ways it bothered me a little that I couldn't comprehend absolutely everything that was being calculated but I did have a general idea of what was going on. As an early childhood teacher, I was well aware of the furore associated with using tests to score the IQ of very young children. There was some furore about IQ measures. However, this was actually one reason I wanted to be in on it because I wanted to look at toddlers' play and see the links between IQ scores, mothers' scaffolding and the children's activity. I wanted to be able to identify the analogical thinking and metacognition and use methods of play that were highly appropriate with young children.

Amy used a longitudinal approach and had the mothers and their children attend once a month, over a nine-month period. The focus was on the mother's scaffolding of their child's play and the sessions were videotaped. Amy reflected: 'It was beautifully rewarding to have these relationships with these mothers and children as part of the data collection process.'

WHAT RESEARCH APPROACHES COULD I CHOOSE?

There are several approaches that can be used to collect data in a quantita-tive study. Some of the methods are similar to those used in qualitative research. However, the methods used generate data that is generally numerically based. Methods can include experiments, sampling, measure-ment and scaling, observation that is more structured and designed to give numerical data, statistical analysis, data reduction, comparative analysis or various forms of surveys. What follows is an introduction to experimen-tal approaches to research and survey research to stimulate your thinking about taking a quantitative approach. We suggest that once you have gained a sense of which approach provides the best fit with your research project, you search out methodology books written specifically about your chosen approach.

Experimental approaches to research

Experimental approaches to research build on the positivist approach (see Chapters 2 and 3) more than any other research technique (Cohen, Manion, & Morrison, 2011). Experimental approaches are best for issues with a narrow scope, being suited for micro- rather than macro-level questions, especially examining effects of causation. Strength exists in the fact that it is possible for you to run many experiments (conducted under laboratory conditions where the variables can be isolated, controlled and manipulated), or quasi-experiments (conducted in the field or natural set-ting, again isolating, controlling and manipulating variables), in a short period. In this type of research your experiment occurs when you modify something in a given situation and then compare an outcome to what existed without the modification (Babbie, 2010). This sees you measure independent variables by creating a particular condition, called an inter-vention or treatment, so that some participants experience one thing and some another. A variable is a factor or item that varies from one case to another, as opposed to a constant that does not vary. Independent variables are input variables which cause an outcome, while dependent variables are outcome variables which are caused by the input (Cohen et al., 2011). Researchers go to great lengths to create an intervention/treatment as they will want this to have an impact and produce specific behaviours and reactions. In fact, the researcher is controlling one or more of the variables while altering the independent variable (Mukherji & Albon, 2010). Dependent variables are the physical conditions, behaviours, atti-tudes, feelings that change in response to the intervention/treatment. An independent variable refers to the cause variable that 'identifies forces or conditions that act on something else' (Neuman, 2007, p. 91) to produce changes.

This research is the strongest technique to use when testing causal relationships because the three conditions necessary for measuring causality – temporal order, association and no alternative explanations – are best met in experimental design. You still need to design research questions or an hypothesis in experimental research and these need to fit the strengths and limitations of the experiment. You also need to be very aware of the ethical and practical implications of intervening in human affairs. The experiment must be limited to the research question(s)/hypothesis where you are ethically and morally able to manipulate and control the conditions (Babbie, 2010).

An early step in your research is to plan the experimental design. You need to decide on the number of groups to be used and also on how and when to create the treatment/intervention conditions. Decisions are also needed on the number of times you will measure the dependent variable. Experiments involve conducting a pre-test, where you measure the dependent variable prior to the introduction of the intervention/treatment, and a post-test, as a follow-up to the treatment/intervention. A simple experiment includes two groups – one that receives the treatment/intervention and one that does not. The group that does not receive the treatment/intervention is known as the control group. After giving the treatment/intervention to one group, you measure the dependent variable and record these measures. You also need to examine the results for each group to test the hypothesis. Ensuring that you can randomly assign (see sampling section below) participants to control or intervention/treatment groups will result in a true experiment.

The control you use in an experiment is crucial as it assists with limiting the alternative explanations to the hypothesis. Researchers sometimes use deception to manage control and you may choose to do this. Deception means that you might intentionally mislead participants in a variety of ways. Deception can make participants act more naturally and can control their understanding of the situation. However, it is important to remember that any means of deception cannot breach the ethics of the research (Neuman, 2007).

Types of experimental research design

According to Neuman (2007) and Babbie (2010), the following are types of experimental design:

- Classical experimental design – uses random assignment, pre-test and post-test, experimental group and control group, and is usually conducted in laboratory conditions (an artificially constructed environment) where the variables can be controlled and manipulated;

- Pre-experimental design – is used in situations where the classical design is difficult. This design makes random assignment and you can use some short cuts. However, there are some weaknesses in this design in relation to inferring causality;
- One-shot case study design – includes one group, a pre-test and a post-test;
- Static group comparison – includes two groups, a post-test and a treatment/intervention. The issue here is that the post-test outcome could be due to group differences;
- Quasi-experimental and special designs – like the classical design, this approach controls, isolates and manipulates variables and is useful when you are seeking to test causal relationships in a variety of situations (in the field or more naturalistic settings);
- Two-group post-test design – groups are randomly assigned and there is no pre-test;
- Interrupted time series – only one group is used, although there are multiple pre-test measures before and after the treatment/intervention;
- Equivalent time series – a one-group design that extends over a time period. It includes a pre-test, treatment/intervention and a post-test, then treatment/intervention followed by a post-test, and so on;
- Latin square design – several treatments/interventions are given in different sequences;
- Solomon four-group design – this design is used when, as a researcher, you believe that a pre-test will sanitise participants to a treatment/intervention and thus improve their performance or change their responses. It combines a classical design with the two-group post-test design. You undertake to randomly assign participants to one of four groups. In this design, two groups receive a pre-test and one of them gets a treatment/intervention and the other an old method. Then another two groups are given no pre-test and one is given a new treatment/intervention and the other the old method. All four groups are given the post-test and are then compared to each other;
- Factorial design – if you choose this design you will use two or more independent variables in combination and will examine every combination of the categories of variables. In the case where each variable contains a multitude of categories, the number of combinations increases. In this case, then, the treatment is not the independent variable but the combination of all of the categories. Various effects result from the way in which this research is implemented.

We hope that by providing these very brief descriptions of different types of experimental research design you will realise the need for further reading in a methodological text devoted to experimental research, if this seems to be the most suitable path for your research.

Survey research

The survey is very widely used as a data-gathering technique in the discipline of sociology and in many other fields. Survey research has its origins in the positivist approach to social science (Ponterotto, 2005). Survey research is most effectively used when the researcher needs to ask questions about an individual's feelings or behaviours and has the strongest results when answers to questions give measurable variables (Neuman, 2007). Surveys allow researchers to ask many questions about many different things and to examine more than one hypothesis at a time. According to Neuman (2007, p. 168), survey researchers 'think of alternative explanations when planning a survey, measure variables that represent alternative explanations (i.e. control variables), then statistically measure their effects and rule out alternative explanations'.

If you want to undertake a survey, you need to begin with a deductive approach that includes a research problem and ends with empirical measurement and data analysis. You must conceptualise the variables as questions so that you are able to gain the responses you need to answer your research questions. The construction of your questions is very important as effective survey questions provide the researcher with valid and reliable measures (Neuman, 2007). Issues such as length, order, order effects, organisation, context effects, format and layout will all have an impact on the design. By piloting the survey you will find out whether the structure of the questions does in fact gather the data that is required for the study. You need to choose questions that work together and that flow smoothly so consider organising them into common, logical themes. The important principles to keep in mind are that questions need to be clear and simple so that participants understand them and give answers that are meaningful. Therefore, it is important to avoid jargon, slang, emotional language, and biased questions (Babbie, 2010). Also, it is important that you phrase questions so that participants do not feel compelled to adhere to stringent social norms (Neuman, 2007). It is always necessary to ensure that participants feel comfortable and not threatened. Try not to ask about intentions in the distant future or use overlapping, unbalanced questions, or double-barrelled questions, and stay away from double negatives (Mukherji & Albon, 2010). With respect to the sequence of the questions, it is necessary for you to order questions to minimise discomfit and confusion (Babbie, 2010). Previous questions can influence the answers to later ones in relation to their content and to previous answers. This can be minimised if you ask general questions first and then move on to more specific ones (Neuman, 2007).

Researchers also need to organise and design questions to assist participants with their own recall. One way of doing this is to provide special instructions and extra time so that participants are able to think through their answers. It is also important for you to avoid dealing with threatening questions too early. Participants can be surveyed via a questionnaire or through a more formal interview process. If asking the questions via an interview, you should give participants a chance to cope with such pressure by allowing sufficient time for them to warm to the task (Babbie, 2010). You should also understand that it is important to develop rapport and create an environment where participants feel comfortable to give honest answers. Thus, it is permissible to build on questions to prompt such responses.

The choice to use open or closed questions, or a combination of the two, depends largely on the purpose and limitations of the research project. Open questions allow the participant to explain their ideas using their own words. Closed questions have a restricted choice of response (i.e. yes/no, true/false), or a Likert scale, which uses either a numerical response (i.e. 1 to 5) or a labelled, graded response (i.e. strongly agree, agree, don't know, disagree or strongly disagree). If you choose to use a numbered response, it is recommended that you signpost the scale, as labelled scales appear to gather a more accurate response. To discover how a participant thinks, feels or believes necessitates the use of open questions, whereas sensitive topics are often best dealt with by using closed questions (Neuman, 2007). On the whole, the use of closed questions requires careful thought and a variety of choices should be offered to cover the scope of answers. The notion of middle positions, such as 'not sure', 'don't know' or 'neutral', can be contentious as well. It is important that you do not take a middle position to mean that the participant does not have a point of view on the subject. Similarly, it is imperative that you do not force participants to take a position when they actually have no opinion on the matter.

The next phase of the survey process is the data collection phase. In this phase you need to contact and coordinate your participants, and it is important for you to keep details of all your participants by tracking them via a numbering process (Lowe, Winzar, & Ward, 2007). This will enable you to transfer information from the survey to a format that can be statistically analysed.

HOW ARE RELIABILITY AND VALIDITY ENSURED WHEN TAKING A QUANTITATIVE APPROACH TO RESEARCH?

Rigorous quantitative research is characterised by appropriate sampling measures, randomised experimental designs with controls, and apt statistical analysis and procedures. Questions around validity in quantitative studies, for example developmental research, relate to measurement equivalence (i.e. is the measure appropriate and accurate across the study – whether that is a cross-sectional or longitudinal study?), cohort effects (is there a difference in participant attributes?), practice effects (is there an impact on changes in behaviour of participants due to 'practising' or becoming more familiar with the tests or measures?), selection bias (are the selected participant groups compatible?), and selection attrition (will the loss of participants skew the data and make the data non representative?) (Hsiu-Zu, O'Farrell, Hong, & You, 2006).

When considering construct validity for quantitative research (i.e. how well a specific measure reflects the theoretical construct it is assumed to measure), the following aspects are applicable:

- content representational (considers the content–item relevance, technical quality and representativeness);
- substantive (theoretical rationales for the process models and engagement by the audience);
- structural (internal structure of assessment tasks supported by theory);
- generalisability (applicability of score interpretations to populations);
- external (relations between test scores and other criteria); and
- consequences (appraisal of perceived and actual consequences of decisions due to the results of the tests) (Crocker, 2006, pp. 379–380).

As Best and Kahn (2006, p. 395) note: 'Tests are often validated by correlating test scores against some outside criteria, which may be scores on tests of accepted validity, successful performance or behaviour, or the expert judgment of recognised authorities'.

Internal validity refers to the strength of the study to stand up to scrutiny. It focuses on the internal logic and consistency of the research. Here the question of how well the findings match reality can be asked. However, if the researcher holds a view that reality is ever changing, then the consideration becomes: 'What seems true may be more important than what is true' (Burns, 2000, p. 476). Internal validity in quantitative research studies is more clearly defined as measuring 'the extent to which the relationships between the variables are correctly interpreted' (Punch, 2009, p. 315). To ensure internal validity of an experiment you will need to have the ability to eliminate alternative explanations for the dependent variable (Neuman, 2007). If you have too many variables, other than the intervention/treatment which can possibly impact on the dependent variable, this can also affect validity. This means that a lot of effort needs to go into ruling out other variables and controlling your conditions. The threats to internal experimental validity are:

- maturation (biological and psychological changes in the participant);
- history (events that may occur between initial and subsequent measuring/ tests/ assessments);

- testing (pre-testing can produce a practice effect);
- unstable instrumentation (unreliable instruments/tools leading to inaccurate and inconsistent results);
- statistical regression (selection of participants with extreme scores at pre-test – either low or high);
- selection bias (non-equivalence of experimental or control groups);
- interaction of selection and maturation (occurs when participants are able to choose which treatment/instructional method they will receive);
- experimental mortality (loss of participants from research study); and
- experimenter bias (influence of researcher's previous knowledge of participants) (Best & Kahn, 2006).

The confidence to generalise to the population is known as external validity and raises the question of generalisability. External validity can be impacted on by reactivity. Reactivity occurs when participants react differently in the research from how they would normally (Cohen et al., 2011). Laboratory experiments tend to have stronger internal validity as it is easier to control variables, but lower external validity and so are less generalisable. Field experiments, which occur in more natural settings than a laboratory, may produce more natural responses but it is much harder to control the variances. This means that the results tend to have greater external validity and lower internal validity. They are more generalisable but less controlled (Neuman, 2007). Like internal validity, there are also threats to external validity. For experimental design studies these threats are:

- interference of prior treatment (effects/impacts of one study may carry over to a new study);
- the artificiality of the experimental setting (sterile/artificial environment may not equal real-life results);
- interaction effect of testing (pre-testing may sensitise participants to the aim of or objective of the study);
- interaction of selection and treatment (if the sample is not a true, randomly selected sample it will impact on the verification of generalisations); and
- the extent of treatment verification (treatment must be administered as intended) (Best & Kahn, 2006).

As previously mentioned, there are also ethical issues relating to placing participants in contrived social settings or in manipulating feelings or behaviour (Neuman, 2007). You should be careful never to place participants in physical danger or in embarrassing or anxiety-producing situations. Chapter 6 provides guidance to ethical practices for researchers.

Like Amy, another researcher, Karen, also used quantitative methods to examine an aspect of young children's behaviour. Karen was curious about children's play. Now a mid-career researcher in the allied health field, Karen recounts her doctoral study experience, where she aimed to develop a standardised, norm-referenced assessment in the area of child-initiated play. As an occupational therapist, she found herself needing to give answers to teachers, parents and other professionals about a child's development while feeling that without an assessment of pretend play, only a partial understanding of the child is gained. Her dilemma, then, became if she was to measure play what would she measure?

After extensive searching of the literature on play, she noted that essential behaviours unique to play, and observed during pretend play, included the use of an object as something else, attribution of a property to an object, and reference to an absent object or 'place'. She therefore embarked on her study, entitled 'The development of an assessment of pretend play', from which she developed the Child-Initiated Pretend Play Assessment (ChIPPA) (Stagnitti, 2003). Developing a new assessment tool involves establishing the reliability and validity of a measurement of a behaviour, set of behaviours or object. As this research was related to the allied health field, the focus was on measuring actions or activities of young children as they engaged with the ChIPPA. This tool assesses the spontaneous ability of young children to organise their play and engage in pretend play. The assessment can be used with children with diverse needs in clinical settings, early childhood settings, schools and homes. It involves a young child engaging with specific play materials, both structured materials and unstructured materials, and having their self-initiated play measured by a trained observer.

Throughout the development of the assessment, reliability and validity were uppermost in Karen's mind. She saw the reliability question as 'How much of the variance in the subject's score is due to the latent variable?' and the validity question as 'Does this assessment measure what it is supposed to measure?'

Karen conducted two studies on the reliability of the ChIPPA, one related to inter-rater reliability and the other examined test-retest reliability. These were chosen because, first, the assessment would be administered by others, so this would depend on an assessor's judgement, and, secondly, the test-retest reliability was important because it provided an indication that the assessment has temporal stability and is less influenced by random changes such as within-subject changes, environment, within examiner changes, the assessment itself, and examiner–subject interaction (Deitz, 1989; DeVellis, 1991). Her validity study looked at discriminative validity. As Karen explains:

I thought that if these three measures (essential behaviours unique to play) are really valuable they should be able to discriminate children who have typical development and children who are suspected as having pre-academic problems. I thought that if this play test can discriminate between those two groups of children then the measures must be really tapping into something that's valuable. I conducted a study involving 82 children (41 typically developing children and 41 where the parent and the teacher were a little concerned about how the child was going to go at school). I looked at the sensitivity and specificity rates and they were really high – they were over 80–85% for sensitivity, which is extremely good, and the discrimination value was really high. I also looked at comparability – looking at how play related to learning, so I had a test for pre-academic skills, which was like the gold standard, which also helped sort the groups out as well.

I also had a place on the scale for concurrent validity, so I looked at how this test related to scales of play and how this related to learning and whether it discriminated between the two groups. I then really drilled down (you know, you are refining all the time) and ended up with a nice refinement of exactly the instructions and exactly the scores. I did another study with 174 children, again looking at whether it discriminated between developmentally delayed children and typically developing children and I also did a test-retest reliability. I thought long and hard about what I was looking at and if it was worth doing a test-retest and I decided it was because if the children were good at organising their play, then they should be good at organising their play over time. In terms of the other validity, like internal consistency, the ChIPPA has two sets of play materials and as the children use them quite differently I did not do this test.

When thinking about advice for beginning researchers relating to validity and reliability using quantitative data, Karen offers the following important comments which could apply to any research project:

They really need to understand the concepts. I think if you understand validity and reliability, you understand that what you're collecting is consistent between you and someone else and that what you are measuring is actually what it is supposed to measure. They also need to understand that validity takes a long time to build up, so I think that novice researchers have to realise that to build up validity around a test you can't just do one research study, you have to do several. I clearly remember my supervisor giving me six books to read on measurement and it took time to get my head around it.

HOW DO I CHOOSE A REPRESENTATIVE SAMPLE FOR MY STUDY?

Quantitative researchers often have to undertake research on a sample of the population rather than the whole population due to access, time and cost. In these cases, a representative sample must be found so that the findings can be generalised to the larger population. There are decisions that need to be made when deciding on the sample, such as:

- the sample size;
- the parameters and representativeness of the sample;
- access to the sample; and
- the sampling strategy (Cohen et al., 2011).

As a quantitative researcher, you begin with the intention to sample a population (Babbie, 2010). A population is an abstract concept, and the researcher has to decide who or what needs to be counted or sampled. The researcher needs to estimate the population to be sampled and then operationalise it by developing a specific list that closely approximates all of the population elements. Neuman (2007) refers to this list as the sampling frame. It is essential that a researcher produce a good sampling frame because mismatches lead to invalid sampling. The researcher has to minimise any sampling mismatches because the sampling frame is crucial to the accuracy of the research.

With any sampling, attention has to be paid to the sample size, which, according to Neuman (2007), depends on three things:

- degree of accuracy;
- degree of variability or diversity of the population; and
- the number of different variables examined simultaneously in data analysis.

The sample size will vary depending on the nature and purpose of the study, the characteristics of the population, the degree of accuracy required and the number of variables needing to be accounted for. If you are in a situation where everything other than the sample is equal, then larger samples are needed for higher accuracy. Smaller samples can be used when less accuracy is thought to be acceptable, when there are fewer variables, or when the population is similar. Sample size can be a contentious issue and each researcher needs to decide on the appropriate size using the rules of research design and statistical analysis.

Probability sampling (random sample) and non-probability sampling are two main methods of sampling. The main difference between the two types is that with a probability sample 'the chances of the members of the population being selected for the sample are known' (Cohen et al., 2011), whereas this is not the case with a non-probability sample.

In quantitative research, the term 'random' has a specific meaning. The random process is one that generates mathematically random results, allowing the researcher to calibrate probability (Neuman, 2007). This means that random samples are most likely to produce a sample that is representative of the population (probability sampling). Probability sampling is based on mathematical processes and so has a level of complexity that allows for sophisticated results. There are a number of different types of probability sample, such as simple random samples, systematic samples, stratified samples, cluster samples, stage and multi-stage samples, and non-probability samples (Cohen et al., 2011). A discussion of some of these follows.

Simple random sampling

A simple random sample is where all members of the population for the study could be selected and by selecting certain members there is no impact on the selection of other members. It is a sample where 'each selection is entirely independent of the next' (Cohen et al., 2011, p. 153). Selection is a random act by the researcher. As you conduct more samples, patterns become more obvious and a bell curve will appear. A bell curve is considered normal distribution for statistics. When normal distribution is plotted on a graph it is bell shaped, hence the name 'bell curve'. According to central limit theorem, as the number of different random samples builds towards infinity, the patterns of the samples and the population parameters become more predictable (Babbie, 2010). However, usually a researcher draws only one random sample and then generalises that sample to the population. Selection can be made through the use of a computer-generated program where each potential participant is assigned a number and the computer program constructs the list of names which becomes the sample, or the names can be randomly drawn out of a hat. In order to apply this method of sampling the whole population needs to be known by the researcher.

Systematic sampling

Systematic sampling is simple random sampling with a modification included for random selection. Researchers number each element in the sample frame by using what is known as a sampling interval (Babbie, 2010). For example, the researcher can choose every third number. In this case, the interval becomes the random method. To apply this method, the sample frame (the order in which the population has been entered to make a list) must have been completed in a random way, otherwise the sample may not be representative.

Stratified sampling

To use stratified sampling the researcher divides the population into sub-groups using extra information (e.g. dividing males and females), thus ensuring that by choosing a random sample from each sub-group a representative sample of the whole population is captured. This type of sampling tends to be more representative than simple random sampling, although the researcher must be able to identify the characteristics of the whole population that needs to be included in the sample.

Cluster sampling

Cluster sampling is applied when the population is geographically spread and large in number, and it is not possible to gain a simple random sample. It involves selecting a number of clusters to represent the overall population of the study. Researchers can randomly assign clusters and sample within these clusters. Once the researcher organises the clusters, he/she is more able to create a sampling frame for elements within the research clusters, making sampling more manageable. Researchers using this method of sampling need to be mindful not to build in bias, which will make the cluster(s) unrepresentative of the population under study (Cohen et al., 2011).

Stage sampling

Cluster sampling can be extended to become what is known as stage sampling. You begin the research with a random sampling of large clusters. Then there needs to be a random sampling of small clusters within each selected larger cluster. You then sample the elements within the sampled small clusters. Thus, you end up sampling the sample. The issue here is that each stage of sampling can produce sampling errors so multi-stage clusters are subject to more sampling errors than a one-stage random sample (Babbie, 2010). You need to address such issues by adjusting the probability or sampling ratio at various stages throughout the sampling (Neuman, 2007). The common factor is the concentration on 'a single unifying purpose throughout the sampling' (Cohen et al., 2011).

Non-probability sampling

Non-probability sampling is used in situations where the sample does not have to represent the population or where there is a particular group that will be the target of the research. Babbie (2010) attests that there are four types of non-probability sampling. These are:

- Reliance on available subjects – this occurs when you simply rely on finding subjects that are available, such as on a street corner or in a shopping centre. There are issues with such a method as there is little control over the situation.
- Purposive – with this method you select a sample based on your knowledge of the population. This is more likely to be considered as a pre-test rather than a field study.
- Snowballing – you can use this method when members of a particular population refer you to other members of that population. As a result, research subjects accumulate via a 'word of mouth' situation.
- Quota sampling – when you use quota sampling you need to begin with a matrix or table that describes the characteristics of the target population. When you have organised your matrix or table, you can collect data from those participants who meet the characteristics of any given cell on the matrix or table. You also need to assign proportion to each cell in relation to the percentage of the total population. Some researchers would argue that quota sampling and snowballing are forms of purposive sampling.

WHAT DO I NEED TO CONSIDER WHEN THINKING ABOUT QUANTITATIVE DATA ANALYSIS?

When analysing quantitative data your attention will be focused on examining 'the distribution of and relationships between the variable under investigation' (O'Hara et al., 2011, p. 197). You may find that you use a variety of different types of statistics, depending on your research questions and the nature of your data. Best and Kahn (2006, p. 354) suggest that researchers ask the following questions in regards to applying a statistical method:

- What facts need to be gathered to provide the information necessary to answer the question(s) or to test the hypothesis?
- How are these data to be selected, gathered, organised and analysed?
- What assumptions underlie the statistical methodology to be employed?
- What conclusions can be validly drawn from the analysis of the data?

Scales of data

To begin, you need to understand the kinds of numbers you are dealing with. These could be nominal, ordinal, interval, or ratio scale. You will have used a nominal scale if you were allocating data into exclusive categories, where set members all have the same defining characteristic, and then counting the data (male/female, socio-economic status, age group, etc.). This data classifies into one category and the categories are 'mutually exclusive and have no numerical meaning' (Cohen et al., 2011).

Ordinal scale, while allocating data to categories, also allows for the ranking of the amount or degree of the differences – i.e. the position or order in the category. 'Ordinal measures have no absolute values, and the real differences between adjacent ranks may not be equal. Ranking spaces them equally, although they may not actually be equally spaced' (Best & Kahn, 2006, p. 290). Rating scales and Likert scales are examples of this.

An interval scale indicates the percentage that a certain characteristic is present. In other words, it introduces a metric – an equal and regular interval – thus, building on the features of both the nominal and ordinal scales (classification and order). However, it lacks a true zero value, which means it does not have the capacity to measure the total absence of a characteristic. Cohen et al. (2011) suggest that in practice this scale is rarely used; the ratio scale is preferred.

A ratio scale has all the features of the previously described scales (classification, order and equal interval properties), but has a true zero, therefore the numerals on the scale have the qualities of the real numbers (time, distance and age). This also allows the four mathematic processes – addition, subtraction, multiplication and division – to be applied to the data. This is considered a powerful method and enables the researcher to easily ascertain proportions (Cohen et al., 2011). Each scale subsumes the previous scale and it is these scales which help the researcher determine which statistical technique to apply.

Types of data

When applying statistical methods, there are two types of data – parametric and nonparametric. Parametric data are measured and assumed to be normally distributed, and can be applied to ratio and interval scaled data. Nonparametric data are counted or ranked using ordinal or nominal scales. It is not assumed that these data are normally distributed across populations.

It is suggested that parametric tests should be used if their basic assumptions relating to the distribution of the population and the way the type of scale is used to quantify data. Best and Kahn (2006, p. 406) list the assumptions for most parametric tests as follows:

- the observations are independent – the selection of one case is not dependent on the selection of any other case;

- the samples have equal, or nearly equal, variances (this is significant for small samples); and
- the variables described are expressed in interval or ratio scales.

Nonparametric tests, which are less precise due to them being based on counted or ranked data, are appropriate when:

- the nature of the population distribution from which the samples are drawn is not known to be normal;
- the variables are expressed in nominal form; and
- the variables are expressed in ordinal form. (Best & Khan, 2006, p. 433).

Mean, median and mode

When working with large statistical data sets, you may find it useful to calculate the most representative number of the data, a central point. To do this you would apply measures of central tendency. Three of the most commonly used measures are the mean, the median and the mode (Burns, 2000).

The *mean* is the sum of all the scores divided by the number of scores in that group. It is the average score within the group and is used to summarise interval and ratio data. Analysis of variance (ANOVA) and t-tests are two ways you can test for differences between the means (average scores) of two or more groups.

The *median* gives the middle value of a distribution when the data is arranged in order from the highest to the lowest value. The median is mainly applied to ordinal data but can also be used for interval and ratio data.

The *mode* is the most frequently occurring value in a set of scores. However, simply using the average, central or most common number within a distribution of data will tell a researcher nothing about the lowest or highest score, or whether there happened to be one very high score in a distribution that held a majority of very low scores. It is therefore suggested that a single measure of central tendency, on its own, is an inadequate way to describe one's data (O'Hara et al., 2011).

When working with the data you may wish to calculate the *standard deviation*. The standard deviation is a reflection of 'the amount of spread that the scores exhibit around some central tendency measure, usually the mean' (Burns, 2000, p. 49), and can be applied when summarising any type of variable.

Levels of analysis

Levels of analysis are descriptive statistics and inferential statistics. Descriptive statistics can be considered as a first-level analysis (O'Hara et al., 2011), where researchers employ methods that allow large numerical data sets to be reduced into more usable formats, such as charts, graphs and tables, which are more easily understood and more accessible. They represent data according to frequencies, averages and ranges (Mukherji & Albon, 2010). They describe and present data (Cohen et al., 2011). They are useful in describing 'the characteristics of the sample in the Method section of your report, check your variables for any violation of the assumptions underlying the statistical techniques that you use to address your research questions, and address specific research questions' (Pallant, 2011, p. 53). The conclusions of descriptive statistical analysis are confined to the particular group under study and are therefore not generalisable – no predictions can be made to the wider population. Parametric descriptive statistics would include mean (average score), standard deviation and Pearson's *r* (which measures the relationship between two measures). Nonparametric descriptive statistics include median (the middle point in the data set), quartile deviation, stanines (a score that divides the normal curve into nine parts), Spearman's *rho* (which measures the relationship between two measures), and mode (the most frequently occurring score) (Best & Kahn, 2006).

Inferential statistical analysis involves the sampling process of a representative group of a larger population, which allows for conclusions to be generalised or inferred from the sample for the larger population. Predictions are made guided by the findings from the data analysis. Parametric inferential statistics would include t-tests (testing the difference between two means), analysis of variance (which determines whether the means of more than two samples are too different to ascribe to sampling error), analysis of covariance (which can remove the effect of a confounding variable's influence), and factor analysis (which condenses variables to more manageable numbers by grouping related items which have aspects in common). Nonparametric inferential statistics include Mann-Whitney (which tests the difference between the ranks of two independent samples) and Chi-square (which tests the independence of the variable – i.e. if the proportions of two or more categories differ from the expected proportions) (Best & Kahn, 2006).

Deciding on the analysis

If your study involves experimental and control group data, you must ensure that you pay attention to the differences between groups and any possible confounding variables. A comparison with a control group that is not subject to a treatment/intervention is essential to determine whether the treatment/intervention did in fact have an effect. Your choice of statistical analysis will depend on whether you have categorical or continuous data or a combination of both, the type of relationship between variables that you wish to examine (correlation, prediction, differences between group means), and the number of independent and dependent variables in your study design. You should be clear about what you wish to achieve from your statistical analysis and the type of analysis you wish to do, to ensure that your study has been designed in an appropriate manner. It is advisable, where applicable, that you choose methods that will enable you to focus on the relationship of variables in your quantitative studies to add depth to your analysis.

What you will find is that computer programs offer a variety of statistical techniques to assist you with your data analysis and will take a fraction of the time it would take you to calculate the answer. A program such as SPSS allows you to undertake many of the statistical analyses mentioned in this chapter. The program instructions will need to be followed regarding preparation of data files and entry, and a check for errors will need to be conducted. Deciding on the correct statistical techniques to apply to your data is perhaps the most difficult part of the research design, so when thinking about using computer analysis programs consider this along with the types of variable that are suitable and which are not. It is also suggested (Pallant, 2011) that you record every session you undertake with the computer program, noting such things as the date, new variables you create, all analyses performed and the file names where the output/results have been saved. Some programs will do this coding for you. If you are studying at a university or large organisation, computer data analysis programs may be available for you to download on to your computer. This is something that is worth checking.

Amy told us earlier about her approach to the research process when she was making decisions about what data to collect and how. In the following section, Amy outlines her method of working and the decisions she had to make regarding data analysis for her research project. It is clear that allocating codes to data is not an easy process, but is one that takes time and much reflection, and Amy saw it as a very exploratory process:

> It's funny because I didn't set out to do this, but even [with] the coding of the play, I actually ended up doing it three times before I fixed on the way I would code things. I'd start out and then by the time I got to the end of the group of children, I'd start thinking 'There's something going on here that doesn't quite fit that sort of coding', so I ended up having two categories, an emerging one and an established code for the play. This came about because I was seeing things that I couldn't say 'Yes, that's definitely this level of play but it looks like the child is almost to that point'. I was using an already available play scale but I adapted it. I added an extra coding for the transformational level of play because I found that the children in my study were all performing certain common, simple transformations and these were happening at an early age, before 12 months. I thought 'Well, I've got to distinguish these from the more

complex transformations and unusual transformations', so I developed a few extra categories. In the end, it didn't really seem to show anything, but I think that was because the children were all so advanced.

Amy took time to think about, and work on her analysis:

> I spent a lot of time and I probably over-complicated it for myself. I questioned whether my analysis was effective in actually producing interesting results. I was always thinking my results would be about levels of play and that the children would be distinguished on the levels of play according to the IQ measures later on. In the end, it wasn't the levels of play that distinguished it; it was what was going on in the zone of proximal development and the scaffolding. So the children were all showing similar levels of play but the children with the higher IQs were receiving, at an earlier point, less scaffolding support from their mothers. There was that earlier transfer of responsibility for the play. So they were all at the same level but the higher IQ children were further along in the zone of proximal development.

One of the hardest aspects for some researchers is to know when to stop analysing the data. Amy found that she had other scaffolding measures that she could have considered but this increased the scale of the research project and took it far beyond the expectations of a doctoral degree. She became overwhelmed as she had become too ambitious. She had six categories of maternal scaffolding and, in the end, she pursued just two. Amy called a halt. To stop other researchers getting into a similar position, she suggests that you 'try and go small and work out what's important. If there's some way you can do a quick review of what you might get, this could act as a useful guide.'

On reading Amy's account of her data analysis, it is interesting to note how she took time to apply different coding frameworks to test what kind of results each would generate. While time-consuming, it enabled Amy to ensure that her findings related directly back to her research questions.

What becomes clear when considering data analysis is that there are certain statistical procedures and types of data, and both should influence your choice of analysis. So when making your choice of which statistical analysis to apply to your data, consider 'the type of question you wish to address, the type of items and scales that were included in your data (questionnaire, survey), the nature of the data you have available for each variable and the assumptions that must be met for each of the different statistical techniques' (Pallant, 2011, p. 106). Cohen et al. (2011) list these considerations as being about the aim of the analysis, 'the kinds of data you are working with (parametric or nonparametric), the scales of data (nominal, ordinal, interval, ratio), the number of groups in the sample, the assumptions of the tests, and whether the samples are independent of each other or related to each other' (p. 697).

The importance of choosing the correct statistical technique to apply to your data is crucial, as the following scenario illustrates. An issue arose in a study which aimed to develop tools to test a positive start to school for children, families and educators. The original aim of the research was to test for face validity and qualitative validity rather than strict psychometric validity and reliability, so the tools (in this case surveys) were designed with this in mind. It was noted at the time that it was unclear whether a high level of psychometric validity and reliability was achievable, not because of the statistics, but more due to the design of the study and the data collection tools. It was decided by another group of researchers to use the data to perform a factor analysis. This was something that the original team of researchers had not taken into consideration in setting up the design or collection phases. This meant that the second group of researchers were trying to extract something that simply was not able to be extracted from the existing data. Issues subsequently arose due to the inconsistencies across the surveys in the way a few of the questions were framed, and this made psychometric validity a problem for those questions (there were surveys to be completed by the child, the parent, and the early childhood and primary school teachers). At the time, this caused tension between the groups of researchers and led to rethinking the choice of analysis. The lesson from this example is that if the data violates the statistical assumptions required to perform a particular statistical analysis, you will need to look for a more appropriate technique to apply.

WHAT DOES TAKING A MIXED METHODS APPROACH MEAN?

A mixed method approach uses multiple forms of data, allowing you to draw on multiple perspectives and possibilities. Mixed method researchers are concerned with pragmatics and diverse data, preferring to use a range of methods to enhance objectivity. A mixed method approach uses both quantitative and qualitative data collection methods and is known by multiple terms, including multi-method, convergence, integrated and combined (Creswell, 2003). According to many researchers, the mixed method approach, which has been around since the late 1950s, is one that has really 'come of age' (Creswell, 2003, p. 4). This approach is used in many of the human sciences today as it is thought that other approaches fall short in many respects, and that the mixed method approach makes up for such shortcomings. The approach is thought to make up for biases in other approaches as it is not subject to the limitations of either quantitative or qualitative approaches. Creswell (2003) states that the need for triangulation of data has assisted in the increased use of mixed method approaches. Triangulation involves the use of multiple and mixed data collection methods to enhance rigour, reliability and validity, thus positioning mixed method approaches as viable options. According to Creswell (2003), there are three general strategies in this approach:

- Sequential – here, as a researcher, you will use one method to enhance the findings of another method. For example, you may begin with a more quantitative method and then follow up with a qualitative method.
- Concurrent – here quantitative and qualitative data converge so that a thorough analysis can be obtained. If you use this method you will collect both forms of data at the same time, integrating the information to interpret the results.
- Transformative – if you use this method, you will use a theoretical lens to view the data. This lens acts as a framework for choosing particular approaches and data collection methods.

Bricolage

One example of this type of transformative approach is called *bricolage*. Lévi-Strauss's (1966, p. 17) notion is of the *bricoleur* as a 'Jack of all trades', who creates patchwork using the different tools, methods and techniques that are at hand. Such an approach deals with the complexity of research and allows the researcher to work within and against (Lather, 1996) competing or overlapping perspectives and philosophies (Stewart, 2001). It is not intended that the pieces of this puzzle will fit together neatly. Rather, the *bricolage* approach assists with the management of disparate data that inform the process of explanation in this case (Macfarlane, 2006). A *bricoleur*, then, requires knowledge of a variety of perspectives and approaches, 'including processes of phenomenography, grounded theory, ethnography, case and field study, structuralism and poststructuralism' (Stewart, 2001, p. 5). What results, is a method that does not offer 'any single model or foolproof approach to discovering the "correct" explanation of problems and differences…' (Riches & Dawson, 2002, p. 210). The theoretical and interpretive *bricolage* reinforces the notion that 'truthful' positions cannot be reached by the use of one perspective (Macfarlane, 2006).

An interpretive *bricolage* is underpinned by the notion that 'research is an interactive process' (Denzin & Lincoln, 2000, p. 9), produced by many aspects of contexts relating to the researcher and to other actors in the process. A combination of interpretive and theoretical *bricolage* allows different theoretical perspectives to inform any investigation and enhances objectivity by recognising how particular aspects of history and context enable and constrain both the process of investigation and the outcome (Macfarlane, 2006). In McLeod's (2000, p. 7) terms the *bricoleur* creates '…

tension between creativity and conformity. The image of the *bricoleur* ... is permissive ... forcing [the researcher] to take higher level epistemological decisions. ... But in many ways this creativity is one of the core characteristics of good qualitative research.' Thus, the use of *bricolage* creates space for an enhanced level of analysis to occur (Macfarlane, 2006).

Bricolage has some detractors in that the method is often criticised as an approach that is used as an excuse for using any theory and literature the researcher wants, regardless of its applicability to the context. Kym, an early career researcher, was part of a research team investigating early childhood leadership using *bricolage*. She argued against the notion that researchers who use *bricolage* do so because their theoretical framework is weak, stating that this is unfounded as the key component of *bricolage* is epistemological coherence. Kym argued:

> A *bricoleur* uses data collection methods, theoretical frameworks and literature that is aligned in ways that allow the data sets in the *bricolage* to be 'sashed' together through the use of relevant theory and literature. I think the *bricoleur* is skilful, as they create a patchwork of information informed by multiple understandings and perspectives. This approach really helped our team to explore leadership in detail, which I think our visual representation shows.

Figure 8.1 illustrates the *bricolage* model and shows how each discrete data set is woven together through the theory and literature that surrounds it.

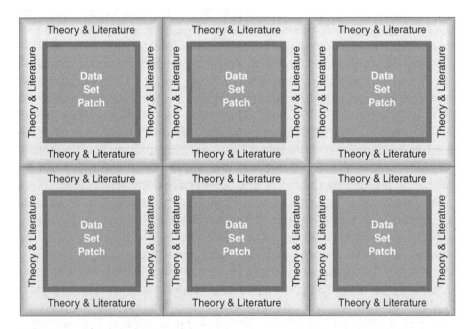

Figure 8.1 The *bricolage* model

HOW DO I GO ABOUT ANALYSING MIXED METHODS DATA?

When undertaking the analysis of a mixed methods study, 'meaningful mixing during the conduct of the analysis' is required (Greene, 2007, p. 143). Greene (2007) views the process of undertaking mixed methods analysis as one of adventure, suggesting that during the analysis stage you build in points where you stop and deliberately look at the data with the intention of finding ways 'in which one analysis could inform another' (p. 144), and searching 'for instances of divergence and dissonance, as these may represent important nodes for further, and highly generative analytic work' (p. 144). Techniques to apply to data analysis have been reported in the literature as including converting the type of data so that all data types can be analysed together, the merging of data to create new data sets, a matching approach where comparisons can be drawn between empirical data and conceptually expected patterns of data, applying aspects of one methodological tradition in the analysis of data from another tradition, and typology development. This last technique is described thus: 'the analysis of one data type yields a typology (or set of substantive categories) that is then used as a framework applied in analysing the contrasting data type' (Caracelli & Greene, 1993, p. 197). Issues relating to the size of the sample and the inclusivity of assigned codes will arise with mixed method analysis.

Work of this type will involve the recoding of your data, with some data being more easily recoded than others. Bazeley (2003) suggests using computer programs that generate concept or network maps as a way to visually represent the data, as this may help bridge issues between taking either a more quantitative or more qualitative approach. What is known is that this type of work is still evolving and by taking a mixed methods approach to your research, you will be at the cutting-edge of informing mixed methods data analysis.

REFLECTION POINTS

If involved in quantitative research using statistical procedures, or a mixed methods approach, consider your responses to the following questions:

- What methodological approach best suits the research question(s) or hypothesis I am trying to answer or address?
- What kind of quantitative methods will gather the data that will be most useful to the research project and how knowledgeable am I about these?
- How am I going to ensure my sample is representative of the population under study?

- How do I plan to safeguard the integrity of my data (i.e. internal and external validity)?
- Do I appreciate the difference between descriptive data analysis and its associated methods and inferential data analysis and its methods?
- How well do I understand commonly used statistical procedures and the logic behind statistical approaches?
- What are the limitations of statistical analysis for my research?
- What would be the benefits of taking a mixed methods approach to my study?

☐ **Summary**

This chapter has focused on quantitative approaches to research and has introduced the associated methodology and methods. Some of the approaches to data analysis have been outlined, providing an overview of commonly used statistical procedures. Also introduced in this chapter is the notion of taking a mixed methods approach to research and what that entails. The main points of the chapter revolve around:

- understanding the differing scales of data, the differences between parametric and nonparametric data, and descriptive and inferential statistics;
- considering the most appropriate approach to take with statistics so the analysis is clear, logical and adds meaning to the research; and
- understanding how mixed method analysis can be applied, resulting in a comprehensive understanding of the phenomenon under study.

9 DRAWING THE JOURNEY TO A CLOSE: DISSEMINATION OF THE FINDINGS

This chapter focuses on drawing the research journey to a close. It presents possible ways for reporting research, including the writing-up process and presenting the findings in a professional manner. Included are brief introductions to the differing types of presentation and what needs to be considered within each approach. Lara recounts her experience of writing up her thesis and the dissemination of her research, especially relating to publishing in peer-reviewed journals. The voices of other researchers are also incorporated into this chapter to provide further practical examples.

Key chapter questions are:

- How do I 'write up' the research?
- What choices do I have in writing up my research and disseminating my research findings?
  - the commissioned research report
  - the thesis
  - the minor project report
  - the academic paper
  - the poster display
  - the oral presentation
  - the book
- What do I need to consider regarding dissemination of my research?
- What part could social media play?
- What is a publication plan and do I need one?

HOW DO I 'WRITE UP' THE RESEARCH?

Even the most carefully planned and executed research will not reach its target if it is not presented accurately, clearly, convincingly, using an engaging but appropriate format. 'It is at the stage of reporting that the quality of the research comes under closest scrutiny and when it will be judged by the wider research community' (Aubrey, David, Godfrey, & Thompson, 2000, p. 179). Therefore, it is imperative that any type of research report must be constructed with care in a systematic way devoid of ambiguities and misinterpretation. What is considered a good overall approach to take when writing up the research is to follow the logical argument that the research presents and to begin writing during the early stages of the research. Punch (2009) suggests considering the research process itself as a set of choices that the researcher has made during the life of the project. It is these decisions that form the basis of the write-up, where they need to be presented as logical and consistent choices after the alternatives have been considered. If you think of research as a journey, as this book is encouraging you to do, then reporting the research can be seen as explaining the path you have taken (Punch, 2009).

It is important to be aware of any accepted style requirements or preferred genres for the format you have chosen. It is also useful to realise that there are certain traditions around reporting. For instance, quantitative research reporting tends to be organised around a structure of the problem, method, results and discussion, whereas qualitative research is more open to other strategies, some of which are discussed below. What you will find is that, as a general rule, research reports comprise a standard format, which begins by introducing the research topic and questions, and moves on to detail the research already known about the topic, the research procedures, the analysed findings, providing a discussion or interpretation of the findings, reflections or recommendations, and ends with a conclusion. The following questions, developed by Taber (2007, p. 187), can act as a guide for you as to the overall structure of a research report:

- Do I want to read this study?
- What is this study about?
- So what do we already know about this?
- So what's the issue/problem here?
- What are you trying to find out?
- How did you go about it (and why)?
- What data did you collect?
- What did you find out (and how do you know)?
- So what?
- Where did you get your background information?
- Where's the evidence?

There are, however, other ways to structure a report. For example, an ethnographic research report tends to be organised around themes that are generated from the field work and data analysis. Reflexivity plays a significant role in the construction of the ethnographic report and involves the 'description and analysis of the research process itself' (Burns, 2000, p. 420). Features of this type of report are the strong use of extracts to represent the data, enabling the reader to understand how the researcher came to the conclusions reported, with a clear articulation of the researcher's roles and positioning within the study. Historical research can also alter the structure, as in this approach the literature review does not stand apart from the data collection or analysis and, as such, cannot be reported separately. Taking a grounded theory approach may also require you to rethink the structure of the report as there is an interplay between data analysis and theory generation, giving it an emergent flavour that may not be captured by the traditional structures of report writing. What you need to understand is that reports can vary from the standard format for good reasons.

Whatever report structure you choose (which may or may not be dictated by the reason for the research – be it an undergraduate minor project, a funded research grant, or a thesis for examination for a higher research degree), begin writing early because you can always go back and edit what you have written at a later stage, when you are perhaps more informed about the research itself and more focused on producing a permanent (often public) record. Don't wait for the perfect opportunity to begin writing, read lots of different styles of writing to gain handy tips, don't edit as you write, and treat writing as a form of thinking. Break a large piece of writing into manageable chunks, share your writing with a trusted colleague or critical friend, draft and redraft, write and rewrite, and edit by ear, which means reading your writing out loud to see if it makes sense and sounds correct (Wellington, 2003). Lara describes the writing-up of her thesis as follows:

> I remember attending a writing skills workshop and then discussing the difference between free writers and people who plan, and I don't plan my writing. I just write. I obviously read back over it, but I don't need to do that (plan). I really enjoy just free writing and that's pretty much how I did most of it. Obviously the chapters were revised but, luckily for me, I did finish and it worked in my favour I think.

By writing as you go, you are better placed to learn from the process itself, with earlier drafts, which are more focused on writing about thinking, developing into more polished pieces of writing that reflect the intent of the project (Mukherji & Albon, 2010). You can more easily recall why certain decisions were made during the research process and the ramifications of these if you capture them as they are happening. For example, Elizabeth Rouse, whose doctoral candidature proposal is featured in Chapter 4, began writing the introduction, literature review and methodology sections of her thesis early on in the research process. While she was immersed in the literature, becoming more informed about her topic ('Effective family partnerships in early childhood education and care – an investigation of the nature of interactions between educators and parents'), Elizabeth was able to construct a first draft of her literature review chapter to the point that she created a model of what the literature regarded as effective family partnerships. She continued on to write a peer-reviewed journal article of her model and understandings of the literature that was accepted for publication.

Beginning your writing early also allows time for you to find your own 'voice' in the writing-up process. The final product, no matter what format, will reflect to the audience your interest in the topic, the decisions you have made within the project, and your discussion and thinking (Mukherji & Albon, 2010, p. 244). If you have embraced a more qualitative approach to your research, then your subjectivity will have impacted on the research in certain ways and this will be reflected in the write-up of your research.

Being conscious of your own voice within the research report also has to be balanced with representing the voice of others – the research participants. Thought must be given to how you are presenting them. Ethical responsibilities are carried right through to the writing-up stage of the research process. These relate to providing a true representation of participants' views or actions, as well as protecting their confidentiality and perhaps anonymising their details. It must be realised that writing-up is not a neutral process (Coffey, 1999).

Taber (2007) challenges researchers to consider effective educational research writing in terms of:

- the literary analogy;
- the legal analogy; and
- the pedagogic analogy.

The literary analogy is the 'story' that acts to lead the audience through the research. There is a natural progression throughout the writing that ensures that the audience reading it understands where the research is going as well as what kind of 'story' is being told. The legal analogy 'makes knowledge claims, and must be able to substantiate them' (Taber, 2007, p. 179). This means presenting a logical and carefully constructed argument supported by convincing and relevant evidence. The pedagogic analogy positions the researcher as a communicator 'informing readers about the research' (p. 179). This is equated to teaching, where attention is paid to the structure, balance and levels of support offered to the audience throughout the writing.

WHAT CHOICES DO I HAVE IN WRITING UP MY RESEARCH AND DISSEMINATING MY RESEARCH FINDINGS?

There are many different ways that research can be disseminated. Some of these include theses, books, book chapters, journal articles, commissioned reports, unpublished research reports, technical papers, conference papers, posters, oral presentations and using social media. Forms such as poetry, film, dance and drama are also acceptable, depending on the purpose of the research and what the researcher is aiming for in terms of distribution of research results. Anne Harris's doctoral research, 'Cross-marked: Sudanese–Australian young women talk education', is one example which applied the principles and practices of ethnocinema. The research explored how students from refugee backgrounds are positioned in their schools and in research, how arts-based methodologies can contribute to changing this positioning, and how practitioners of the emerging practice of ethnocinema as a research methodology cannot escape the process unscathed. Anne's research was represented by seven documentary films which comprised comment on the complexities of the identities for both researcher and co-participants. Six of these films were the participants' and one was the researcher's, and all of them were created collaboratively. The films were accompanied by a text (thesis) which has subsequently been published (Harris, 2011).

Following is a brief outline of some forms of dissemination and the structure and process that is required for each.

The commissioned research report

If you have undertaken commissioned research, the shape of the report will be determined by the funding body brief, which usually encompasses detailing the project brief, how the research was conducted, the findings and the implications of the findings, which usually comprise recommendations for action or change. A conclusion for this type of report must relate back to the original brief of the project, drawing attention to how the aim has been met. This is then followed by the implications, often presented as recommendations, which flow from the findings. The final report should assure the funding organisation that the research was of a high standard, and that the outcomes match the stated deliverables, illustrating that the money was well spent. There may be issues around you publishing from this research due to owner-ship of the intellectual property. This issue needs to be sorted before you sign the contract to undertake the research.

The thesis

A thesis is written with the specific aim of being awarded a higher degree. It can be considered as an examination piece of writing. Each institution will have developed a format detailing how the thesis should be presented and you will need to become familiar with this and tailor your presenta-tion accordingly. When producing a thesis, there is a fairly standard structure/format to follow. Generally speaking, it should be seen as a well-constructed, logical argument for your research project. Burns (2000) views the process of writing up a thesis as moving from the general to the specific in the introductory chapters, then moving from the specific to the general in the discussion and concluding chapters. The standard structure is: title page, candidate's statement, acknowledgements, abstract, table of contents, introduction and background to the research, including the research question(s), a review of the related literature, procedures applied to conducting the study (methodology), the study findings, a dis-cussion of these findings in light of the known literature and the new knowledge generated from the study, limitations of the study, a conclusion, references, appendices. The number of chapters and word length dedicated to each aspect of the study will be determined by the type of research and the academic level of the thesis, i.e. honours, Masters or doctoral. Each of the above-mentioned sections or chapters are now discussed in more detail.

Title

Along with the abstract, the title is important as it impacts the indexing system for the research literature. It needs to capture the nature of the research so that those who are searching databases for literature on a topic will come across your contribution.

Abstract

This is a summary of the research project. Kamler and Thomson (2006) consider abstracts as 'tiny texts' as 'they compress the rhetorical act of arguing into a small textual space using a small number of words. But they are "large" in the pedagogical work they can accomplish' (p. 85). An abstract needs to address the aims of the research and how this has been investigated, along with the findings, and situates the study within the field. It is recommended that you, first, situate the research issue(s) within the broader context, drawing on the literature for support, and then move on to outlining your study. Next, report your findings and then argue why these are significant. Applying the 'Four Moves' strategy (Kamler, 2010) – locate, focus, report and argue – will help you organise the type of information that needs to be included in an abstract and a possible order for how that information appears.

Punch (2009) describes good abstract writing as 'saying as much as possible in as few words as possible' (p. 337). Some researchers suggest writing the abstract first, while others leave it until last. It does depend on how you like to work and whether or not writing it first (and leaving space where the not yet known findings will be inserted at a later date) will act as a guide to your overall writing. For example, when writing a journal article, it is a common practice that the abstract is written first to provide the framework around which the article can be structured. Genre questions developed by Kamler and Thomson (2006, p. 88) will assist you to think critically about your abstract. These questions are:

- What is the research problem being addressed?
- How do I locate the significance of my work?
- What conversation am I in? Where am I standing in relation to research on this problem?
- What do I offer as an alternative to existing research?
- What is my argument?

Murray (2009) suggests the use of Brown's (1994) eight questions to help structure your ideas and provide a framework for writing an abstract. These questions are:

- Who are the intended readers? List 3–5 names
- What did you do?
- Why did you do it?
- What happened (when you did that)?
- What do the results mean in theory?
- What do the results mean in practice?
- What is the key benefit for readers?
- What remains unresolved?

Introduction and background

Like the abstract, it is suggested that you begin with a statement about the core issue of study, locating it within the context and literature. This should then lead to the situating of the research itself and what is to be investigated. The use of sub-headings, which act as signposts for the reader, is an accepted practice in this section. This section should answer the following questions for the audience/reader:

- Why did the researcher choose to study this topic?
- What is already happening in relation to the chosen topic?
- What is the aim and purpose of this study?
- Why is this study significant?
- How is the report organised? Where will I locate certain information in the report?

Andrea's research, entitled 'The state of play in early childhood teacher training in Victoria', began with her locating her own interest in the topic of early childhood teacher education and her own related experience of teacher training. Under the next sub-heading 'A statement of aim', she detailed the aim and purpose of her study and then continued to discuss the significance of the study to the field of early childhood education and higher education. Also included here were the research questions. The last section of this introductory chapter was devoted to informing the reader about the structure of the report, such as where information about certain aspects of the research process was located. Andrea's thesis used a standard format approach for a doctoral thesis.

Literature review

The literature review was discussed in detail in Chapter 5 so we will just say here that this can take up more than one chapter of your thesis, depending on the extent and varied nature of the literature related to the study or the type of study you undertook.

Methodology

Particular attention is required for the methodology section where detailed writing about the research process is undertaken and justified. This section is totally focused on the design of your study. To check if you have provided enough detail in this section and have included everything that is needed, ask yourself: If someone wanted to replicate your study could they do so from the information you have provided? Also consider whether you have presented this information in a clear, concise and systematic way. If you are applying test instruments, or using surveys, or interviews, they will need to be detailed in this section, along with a description of the conditions under which these were administered. A blank copy of any instruments or tools used in your research should be attached as an appendix and the reader can be referred to the appendix attachment(s) in the body of this methodology chapter. Readers should be able to answer the following questions after reading a methodology section:

- What methodology was applied?
- Who took part in this study?
- How were they enlisted?
- What form did this participation take?
- Were any other methods of data collection utilised?
- How was the data managed?
- How was the data analysed?
- How was validity and reliability ensured?
- What were the limitations of the methodology and methods?
- How were these limitations compensated?

Results/findings

The results section should showcase your findings in a way that illustrates the complexity and richness of them. In representing your research and its findings you must ensure that you choose the best possible method to report this information. Keep in mind your research question(s) or hypothesis and use this to organise the section. Using sub-headings will provide a way to organise your data rather than trying to present too much at once, which can be overwhelming and confusing for someone reading your thesis. Presenting too much at once is a common problem, especially related to using graphs, which can become too overcrowded and make interpretation difficult (Burns, 2000). If using features such as graphs, tables, histograms, scatterplots, box plots or illustrations, it is good practice to discuss and comment on these either in the paragraph preceding the visual or directly after it. This adds clarity to what the visual is highlighting. However, do not use visuals just for the sake of it as they may not capture the richness of the data you want to report.

Discussion

Burns (2000) stance on the structure of the discussion section of a thesis is that it should incorporate a restating of the questions or hypotheses and findings, the linking of results to previous research and theory, and provide broad implications, methodological implications and directions for future research. This part of the thesis should address questions such as:

- How do the findings relate to my research question(s) or hypothesis?
- How do they compare to previous research and theory on the topic/issue?
- What are the ramifications of these findings?

- What were the limitations of the study findings?
- What other questions does this research raise for future research opportunities?

Conclusion

The conclusion should act as a summary of the research project, outlining the broader ramifications the findings may have for the 'worlds of ideas and action they affect' (Punch, 2009, p. 338).

The minor project report

The structure of a minor report (which may be an undergraduate project) may mirror the structure of the thesis. The difference is mainly in the size of the report, and the amount and depth of detail expected, especially around the scope and breadth of the study and level of analysis. At undergraduate level, more directions are usually provided to students to guide them as to how many words are expected in each section of the report and the overall expectations to be considered in the assessment process. There may also be the opportunity to view past minor project reports to gain a sense of what one looks like.

The academic paper

It is argued (Aubrey et al., 2000) that a measure of quality research is having your research published in a prestigious, peer-reviewed journal as these serve as gate-keepers. What needs to be considered when writing a paper is the intended audience and whether your topic falls within the scope of the conference (for Conference Proceedings) or journal. Papers are usually about theory generation or innovative ideas or new knowledge, and are usually a direct result of completed research projects or theses, but this is not always the case. While following a similar structure to that of a thesis, an academic paper is much shorter in length and, as such, has to be more concise.

Christine, when discussing her first attempt at developing a journal article from her doctoral thesis, recalls this as being a completely different process from writing a thesis. 'I just did not know how to go about it. What I produced was a mini copy of my thesis in a few thousand words. This meant that nothing could be dealt with in any depth as I tried to cover everything that I had raised in the thesis.' Her first attempt was to present the article as a summary of her entire thesis which, with hindsight, she realised was not a wise move, as to cover such a body of work in one article is not possible. At the time, the letter of rejection was devastating for Christine and she put the article aside, not knowing how to deal with turning her thesis into publications. Through experience, Christine learned to narrow the focus, choosing an aspect of her research that would be of interest to the journal's readers and presenting this as an article.

A successful article requires a brief presentation of the literature to situate the study, a more detailed overview of your own study, and the findings and discussions. Working in this way, a more in-depth examination of a particular aspect can be presented. For instance, some higher degree research students can have three or more articles published on various aspects of their thesis, such as the literature review, methodology, and the findings. As a higher degree student, you will need to ask your supervisor, or check with your institution, about the protocols surrounding publishing papers while undertaking your thesis. For some disciplines it is accepted practice for the student to co-publish with their supervisor, although this does also depend on the wishes of the supervisor in question and the policy of the institution. What has to be considered is how the supervisor's contribution to the production of the knowledge behind the paper has influenced the finished product.

Sometimes it is a good idea to begin by co-publishing with a more established researcher who will be able to guide you through the process. When writing a joint paper it is usually the researcher who initiates the idea of the paper and who takes up the role of lead author. This means taking on a substantial amount of the work and coordinating the effort. Before starting off on this venture, it is important to establish a protocol about each researcher's input and thus the order in which the authors will appear on the published paper. If this is not decided at the beginning of the collaborative writing process, it can make for an uncomfortable situation at the end of the writing period when colleagues defend their rights as to where they think they should be positioned in accordance to their perceived effort on the production of the paper.

The poster display

If you want to represent your work using a visual, static medium, consider a poster presentation. A poster can be a very effective way of informing others about your research as often posters are placed in prominent places where people congregate and remain in place for the life of the event, which contrasts to a time-limited, one-off oral presentation. This is also an option for those new to presenting research findings, who may become nervous at the thought of standing up at a conference delivering an oral presentation. Some conferences will ask presenters to change from an oral presentation to a poster presentation if the number of participants wanting to present is greater than the time available.

Your poster should revolve around the core issue of your research, a central message, the research question or hypothesis, and the questions which test this hypothesis. Think about your poster in the same way you think about a paper because the same sections need to be included but in a more condensed, and thus concise, way. Sections should include:

- a summary of aim(s)
- an introduction and background section
- the methodology or theory
- the results
- a discussion
- a conclusion or section detailing the significance of your research
- references.

Highlight in each section only the main points. The American Society of Primatologists suggests that you apply the 25-words-or-less exercise to each section. This method asks you to describe your central message in 25 words, your introduction in 25 words, your methodology or theory in 25 words, and so forth. While this can be difficult to do, it will guarantee you a poster that is not so crammed with text that it becomes cumbersome in presentation and difficult to read. You must edit ruthlessly. Other restrictions that need consideration are whether there is a preferred poster size, the size of the available space you have been allocated, and whether a poster is a suitable vehicle to represent your research.

When constructing your poster, be mindful that it will be read from a distance so you will have to enlarge the print size. Use clear headings by which to organise your information and consider using bullet points which can then be elaborated in a following paragraph. The colour of the backing paper and use of colour within the poster itself also need to be tested because some coloured print is almost impossible to read on certain coloured backdrops. We have seen many undergraduate students using yellow text because it looks bright, yet from a distance it cannot be read. Limit the amount of colour in the text as this can be overwhelming and distracting; instead use colour effectively to highlight important points or different sections.

Don't discount the use of visuals on the poster. Consider incorporating tables, flow charts, graphs or photographs, as appropriate, but again don't overdo their usage and make sure they are of a high quality so they don't detract from the overall presentation. Some presenters provide handouts to accompany the poster which can provide more detailed information. These can sit in an envelope attached to the side or bottom edge of your poster or sometimes can be displayed on a table under your poster. It will depend on the space you are allocated. Experience shows that you can become so absorbed in your construction of the poster that you fail to see typos such as spelling errors or information aligned under incorrect headings. To alleviate this problem, ask your colleagues to review your work to make sure the overall presentation is of a high standard and properly showcases your research.

The oral presentation

When preparing for an oral presentation, take time to think about what you want to achieve. The answers to the following questions will help you shape your presentation:

- Who is the audience and how informed are they already about your topic and your research?
- What is it that you want the audience to understand or learn about your research?
- Do you want to present your results for further consultation with the audience or as a *fait accompli?*

Kristy, a member of a research team undertaking a large government project relating to positive transitions to school for children, families and teachers, was asked to present the findings at a local preschool Annual General Meeting. Due to the type of event and the composition of the audience (mainly parents of preschool children), her presentation was focused on the practical aspects of the findings so that the parents could identify with the indicators that the study developed and apply them to their own situations. There was no need on this occasion to present a more typical research report presentation, as expected at academic conferences, because while the methodology and methods were briefly outlined, it was the practical application that interested this audience. If choosing to present at a research conference, your approach would be very different and you will find that your abstract will make a good basis on which to plan your presentation, especially if using Kamler's (2010) four moves – locate, focus, report and argue. Some conferences welcome the presentation of 'research in progress' because it allows the researcher to test his/her developing ideas and theories and receive feedback.

When presenting, be aware that you should plan your time carefully as quite often presenters run out of time before they have had a chance to outline the significance of the findings for the field or practice. For any presentation, the key is to practise to ensure you become familiar with what you want to say and can pace your presentation, as there is usually a time limit for how long you have to speak. Remember that less is more. You want to leave time to conclude with a clear summary of what you have covered and to take questions and comments from the audience. It is these questions and comments that can help you clarify points which may not have been clear in the initial presentation.

Try to begin with something that will capture the attention and interest of your audience. One way to do this is to accompany your oral presentation with visual aids, such as using PowerPoint software. Using a photograph, picture, cartoon or artefact related to your topic can be a good way to begin, or you may like to start by putting forward a question that will make the audience think. It is always good practice to inform the audience of the purpose of the presentation and what you intend to cover. Making the data 'come alive' so audience members can engage with it can be accomplished by the use of extracts from the data or artefacts, so choose data that provide clear examples to help illustrate the points you are making. If using visual aids, consider them as supplementing visually what you are saying orally. Handouts with key points and related information are a useful way to include more detailed information than is possible in an oral presentation. However, you will have to decide if you want the audience members to have the handouts before or after your presentation.

The book

You can either be approached by a publisher to write a book or you can actively pursue this avenue yourself. Whichever way you go, before you receive the go ahead to begin the writing process you will need to submit a proposal to the publisher. Publishing houses tend to have their own book proposal guidelines, but as a rule they encompass sections such as:

> **The text and its purpose** – In this section you provide the proposed title and author(s) name(s) as well as an outline as to the type of book you propose (textbook, supplementary textbook, monograph, handbook). A synopsis of the book, including the topic, purpose, scope and length (number of pages or word count), will also be required.

> **Features of the text** – Pedagogical features that will be included in the book (checklists, a glossary, learning outcomes, examples, summaries, case studies, suggested readings, references, a bibliography, appendices, self-assessment or reflection questions, introductions to chapters, end-of-chapter summaries, etc.) need to be noted, along with other features such as graphics (tables, graphs, maps, photographs) and any supplementary features (software, study guide, practitioner's manual).

Outline – Provide a 'Table of Contents' where you give an overview of each chapter's content, including sub-headings. Note what you consider to be important or unique features in each chapter.

The market – Here you list the competing titles already on the market and compare these with your proposed text. This could include a strengths and weaknesses assessment of the direct competitors. Also in this section, you will need to detail who would be the likely reader of the book (the primary market), the secondary market, the scope of the market (national, international), provide a sense of the current marketplace and any perceived future changes, and the currency of the text. You could also be asked to provide an estimation of sales.

Schedule – A timetable for completion of the manuscript (completion of individual chapters so these can be sent out for review as well as the delivery of the final manuscript) is what is required in this section.

Reviewers – You may be asked to suggest suitable reviewers for the manuscript and you may even have the opportunity to note who should be avoided as a reviewer.

Author(s) – Here you include your up-to-date curriculum vitae and the names of people who could act as referees to support your proposal.

Preparing a book proposal takes time, thought and research into the intended marketplace and competing titles already in existence. Before a decision to go ahead is given, this proposal will be sent out for review to people already working in the field for their assessment of its currency. You need to think carefully before venturing down the book publication path as not all publishing houses are concerned with quality or the integrity of your research, instead privileging the saleability of the end product. Do your homework on the history of the publishers to find out the 'best fit' for you to disseminate your research findings. For example, there are difficulties in trying to sell a very scholarly book to a publisher which is more concentrated on marketing widely (Yates, 2005). The topic, timing and presentation of the book require careful consideration to be attractive to a publisher and the wider marketplace, as well as true to your original research or intent.

WHAT DO I NEED TO CONSIDER REGARDING DISSEMINATION OF MY RESEARCH?

There is much to contemplate when it comes to the dissemination of your findings. You must consider the audience you are targeting and how they can best access the information. This involves not only locating the information but also in understanding and engaging with it. Informing the research participants of the outcomes of your research project is considered part of taking an ethical approach to your role as a researcher (see Chapter 6). This does not have to be a long, detailed report and can be as brief as a newsletter or report summary. The form that this takes, as well as the sensitivities surrounding this process, will have been detailed in your ethics application submission. Keeping your participants informed and providing them with feedback is one way to ensure that, should you require them to participate in another of your studies, they may be willing. Kellett (2010) makes the point that feedback of results should not be excluded from child participants as they have just as much right to be informed as do adult participants. This is one aspect that can be overlooked when planning the dissemination of findings.

WHAT PART COULD SOCIAL MEDIA PLAY?

While a relatively new phenomenon in relation to research, social media can offer a number of benefits. Benefits include the efficient, effective, widespread dissemination of information through the various tools it offers. Social media has the ability to open up your research to a new audience in flexible and responsive ways. When considering whether or not to communicate your research through social media tools such as blogging, microblogging, wikis, widgets, social news, live streaming, message boards, chat rooms, podcasts, video sharing, photo sharing and virtual worlds, the following questions, as developed by Cann, Dimitriou, and Hooley (2011, p. 21), should guide you:

- What is the appropriate tone for publication of scholarly ideas via social media?
  - Do I write as if I were producing a conventional academic article or do I need a different approach?
- What should I publish and when?
  - Do I wait for things to be published in academic journals or can I start dissemination earlier?
- Are there intellectual property and copyright implications if I make ideas and results available using social media?
- Who is my audience?

It is suggested (Cann et al., 2011) that each decision about questions such as these is personal and relates to the nature of the research project.

Consider the goals you are hoping to achieve by using social media to disseminate your research to your target audience. One size does not fit all, so carefully consider the online habits of your potential audience in order to maximise the effectiveness of this form of communication. You will need to be selective. If you are a higher degree by research student, you are strongly advised to discuss the use of social media with your supervisor before choosing to go down this path. It is up to each researcher to consider the implications of using social media and the impact this will have on the dissemination of the research.

If you do decide that social media is a viable option for you, you will have to develop an online environment that is attractive, easy to find and easy to access (e.g. which is easy to open, scan and print). The values need to be immediately identifiable, summaries need to be clustered for ease of viewing, the relevance must be obvious, and the text concise. Remember that social media can generally be read by anyone and this may impact on what you choose to write and the way you write it. While there are credibility issues associated with using social media (there are no gatekeepers and your work may be judged not on its substance but rather on the visual appeal of the site), make a concerted effort to represent your information in a format that cannot be manipulated or distorted by users' hardware. Electronic journals and social media are changing the way we connect, so do track if it is working for you by keying into programs that provide you with feedback, such as alerts.

WHAT IS A PUBLICATION PLAN AND DO I NEED ONE?

When considering the dissemination of your research it is good practice to develop a Publication Plan where you decide what aspects of the research would make interesting reading for particular audiences, how to present them in an engaging way, and which journals might support the themes of your work. This plan will help you to see that dissemination of research is an ongoing process that takes many forms in order to reach a wider audience than perhaps was the original intention of the study. Drawing up a table where you can track your publication ideas and progress is often a useful exercise (see Table 9.1).

Table 9.1   Publication Plan template

Details of writing project	Idea for written piece: Invitation Research grant Research report Proposal	First draft	Working draft being read by colleagues	Submitted to targeted journal (name)	Re-drafting after peer-review	Resubmitted	Accepted for publication	Proofs to correct	Publication (date)

Lara recounts her publishing aspirations in the following excerpt, where she begins by suggesting that other beginning researchers develop a Publication Plan:

> I would suggest that others develop a plan. I mean, I had it in my diary that I was going to work on writing for publication, you know, this fortnight, while my thesis was off being read by someone. I didn't really stick to that, that much. I did write and get published, but it was in non-peer-reviewed journals because I wanted to write for informed practice rather than for an academic audience purely. If it's someone who enjoys writing, do it because it's a break in a way, and you consolidate your thoughts. And maybe even as a really good exercise, imagine you have to write a journal paper and you can only refer to a very small section of your findings, how would you do that? Does it stand up?

This reflection illustrates the difficulties that some researchers new to publishing can encounter. Lara is truthful about her own understandings of the process and the limits of these understandings and how there were essential skills that she now realises are required for the successful dissemination of research.

REFLECTION POINTS

When considering the dissemination and write-up of your research, reflect on the following questions:

- How do I capture the essence of the research as it unfolds?
- Who is the target audience?
- What is the best way for this audience to understand and engage with my research?

- How do I plan to ensure the confidentiality and anonymity of the research participants when disseminating my findings?
- What are the style requirements and preferred genres of the method of dissemination I have chosen?
- Have I looked at other research projects that have applied this method of dissemination so I am knowledgeable about the tradition that surrounds this method?

Summary

This chapter has focused on disseminating research results expounding possible ways to present the findings in a professional manner which allows the richness and complexity of the research to be displayed. It reminds the researcher to begin writing early on in the research process and to write in a clear, concise and logical way. Other aspects considered include:

- following the structure of the chosen method for dissemination;
- considering ethical implications of reporting findings relating to the lives of participants; and
- developing a publication plan to ensure that dissemination of the research is an ongoing process.

10 THE JOURNEY

Reflecting on the journey is an important part of the research process, not only in helping you to understand what your research may have achieved, but also in gaining a sense of oneself as a researcher. This chapter highlights how a person may develop throughout the process and suggests ways to further advance research skills and practice for the future. Being part of a research community presents challenges and benefits, so this chapter will also address what these might be in a localised community. The chapter concludes with the voices of Amy and Lara, whose journeys we have followed throughout this book. They summarise their own initial research journeys and plot the course ahead.

Key chapter questions are:

- How might the research process impact on my development as a researcher?
- What impact could research communities have on my development as a researcher?
- How do I reflect on my experience so that I can become more self-aware as a researcher?
- What impact could my research have…

    ○ …on my own practice and the practice of others?
    ○ …on policy development?

- Where to from here?

HOW MIGHT THE RESEARCH PROCESS IMPACT ON MY DEVELOPMENT AS A RESEARCHER?

There is no doubt that being involved in research does impact on you at an individual level, both personally and professionally. Whether you have completed research by yourself or in a team environment, you may have had opportunities to build your research expertise, confidence and sense of accomplishment. If you have been exposed to new methodologies and methods in undertaking the research project, this will have increased your understanding of working with different ideas in different ways. Research is a journey as well as a process. Lara reflects on her development as a researcher thus:

> I think I feel like I am an independent researcher now and absolutely I wasn't before. While I was doing it, I always thought at the time 'They don't train you to do interviews. They don't train you to do this.' They give you how to manage a project and different reference software and things like that. But they don't train you in research skills... but you learn by doing. So you are going to develop those skills by doing it. They may not be as perfect as they could be, but by doing it you will learn them and obviously now if you go into research, then you've got those skills.

Throughout the journey, take note of what you are experiencing, such as the processes you are involved in and how confident and comfortable you are in applying these. You will be able to use these notes to reflect on your development as a researcher at some point in time. By taking note of how you have contributed towards the research project – conceptualising the project, designing the data collection tools, liaising with the colleagues in your field or discipline, gaining ethical approval, collecting the data, analysing the data, writing the report and so on, can become your personal record and be added to your curriculum vitae and research profile.

When we asked Amy about her own development during the research process she responded by seeing herself as being quite courageous in undertaking the thesis journey:

> One thing stands out to me and that is I think I'm quite brave. I think now I look back, it was quite brave. People said 'You can't do it' – foolish, I suppose. Some people would say 'foolish'. But I suppose I was quite amazed that I could pursue it, particularly taking so long and not having a full-time academic job, being part-time, sessional work or what not. You know, questions come up from within me and from family and friends. 'What are you doing? Is this really the right thing to be doing – spending this much time of your life on this?' But I think I knew in the end it was worth it.

WHAT IMPACT COULD RESEARCH COMMUNITIES HAVE ON MY DEVELOPMENT AS A RESEARCHER?

Lara described her research community as follows:

> It was very culturally diverse and very age diverse and probably male-dominated. It was an audiology biomedical sciences and speech language therapy group so I was probably among the few qualitative researchers, plus I was doing field work.

> Everyone else was laboratory based, so there wasn't really that much of a way to connect with people. I felt that I didn't really want to be at the university that much, so I wasn't really looking for friends in that respect.

Being a young, female student taking a more qualitative approach than the other students meant that there were limited connections between Lara and the other student researchers. As Lara suggests: 'But what I really needed, I think, were like-minded people.' Burton and Bartlett (2005, p. 2) consider that 'communities of like-minded practitioners can share their experiences and extend their understanding in international as well as very local contexts'. Electronic communication is a powerful aid to enable this to happen on a more global scale. Therefore, it is important for any researcher, whether a novice or more experienced one, to establish a network of researchers who share similar beliefs, practices or understandings, or who have a healthy respect for each other's diverse views and methodologies. While there is no need to be actually researching together on a project, this network can be utilised as a 'sounding board' or group of 'critical friends' to stimulate your thinking about possible research endeavours and may join with you at times to undertake collaborative research projects.

Working with researchers from other disciplines outside your own allows you to recognise that other researchers prioritise different aspects of research, for example, statistics, quantitative approaches, qualitative approaches. One researcher, Ali, an early career researcher at the time, recounts his experience of being part of a large evaluation study where educationalists and healthcare professionals came together to ensure that children's holistic development (education, health, welfare) was taken into account in the project. Right from the start, the methodology and methods were different from what he had become used to utilising. Working within this team took courage as Ali was challenged many times about the robustness of his more qualitative approach. He had to defend his stance within the project with those taking a more positivist approach, who were relying heavily on statistics. The end result was a comprehensive government report which was able to present detailed statistics but with the narratives of the participants' lives intertwined to showcase the story behind the facts and figures. While the research journey was challenging, and at times uncomfortable for the researcher, so much so that at a number of points in the project he wanted to cease his involvement, persevering gave him a greater understanding of his colleagues' priorities and a way forward to mesh both quantitative and qualitative methods in producing a detailed report.

On a personal level, participation in projects like Ali's open up possibilities for considering other methodologies that are unknown at the time.

As one researcher, who was invited to join established researchers from other disciplines on a research project, exclaimed: 'I feel totally out of my depth!' It is at times like this that you may need to reflect on why you are feeling this way. If you can recognise the triggers to these feelings of inadequacy, perhaps you can begin to plan to address them by considering what you bring to the project. If you have been invited to join a project, there is usually a reason why this has occurred, so perhaps it is this that you have to determine to help you feel more at ease.

HOW DO I REFLECT ON MY EXPERIENCE SO THAT I CAN BECOME MORE SELF-AWARE AS A RESEARCHER?

A telling moment when interviewing researchers for this book was their delight at being asked to tell the story of their own research journey – the good, the bad and the ugly! They relished the chance to reflect on the experience, taking time to contemplate and ponder their own personal journeys, rather than just reporting on the research findings. Undertaking research does have a personal impact on you, the researcher, and you need to take time to consider this impact on you, your work, the field in general, and the ramifications this has for future research possibilities. Researchers can be so caught up meeting deadlines and milestones, working towards the completion of their research project, that they do not spend time reflecting on the journey itself. However, the process of reflection, throughout your research journey, allows you to become more self-aware along the way.

Reflection, as a process, is defined in slightly different ways in the literature, although there are common elements. These include the exploration of experience, the analysis of feelings to inform learning, elements of critical theory, and changed action or perspective (Bulman, 2004). Dewey (1933) defined thinking reflectively as 'active, persistent and careful consideration of any belief or supposed form of knowledge in the light of the grounds that support it and further conclusions to which it tends' (p. 9). This means thinking with a purpose. There needs to be a commitment to reflect on the personal and professional journey experienced in order to develop a greater understanding of your research abilities and skills and how these can be further developed in the future. To get the most out of the process, reflection needs to be a deliberate, conscious and ongoing act throughout the research project.

One way to begin the reflection process is to take note of your learning and the challenges you have faced during your journey. Keeping a personal diary or journal ensures reflection throughout the whole process. If issues are concerning you, note these down, because by trying to understand why these issues concern you, and all their complexity, you might be able to work to change the situation. Being reflective and reflexive enables us as researchers to examine how our research might impact on society and how the society might impact on our research (Hand, 2003). A group of undergraduate students undertaking action research projects found that using a research journal a useful reflective tool. The journal helped them to clarify their thoughts relating to both the research process itself and their own feelings of becoming a researcher. Their comments were candid but truthful accounts of the frustrations, fears and joys they experienced as they struggled with taking on the role of a researcher for the first time. What was very noticeable during the life of their research journeys was the growth in understanding and positive engagement with the research process and a respect for how this could be harnessed to inform their daily professional practice.

Through reflection, you will come to understand and locate yourself as a researcher. However, locating yourself as a researcher may take time and develop over many projects. It must also be realised that, in relation to education researchers, they are often 'hybrid workers' (Yates, 2005, p. 207) as organisations such as universities and government departments require individuals to work across a range of different research forms (Gibbons, Limoges, Nowotny, Schwartzman, Scott, & Trow, 1994; Scheeres & Solomon, 2000). Your personal research identity will be shaped by your research experiences and will be informed by reflecting on the decisions you make regarding the methodologies that you become more comfortable applying. It will provide you with a sense of who you are as a researcher within the research community. Safira, an experienced researcher, reflects:

> I keep learning new things from each project I undertake as I work with different colleagues who bring different methodologies and understandings of what research should and could look like to the research project. While I feel comfortable researching in certain ways, I am often stretched to consider other ways of knowing and doing that take me outside my comfort zone. This is challenging, yet exciting and stimulating.

You may like to ask yourself the following questions to begin thinking about your own research identity:

- How do I position myself as a researcher? Why?
- What theories have influenced my practice and research?

- Would I feel comfortable using other research methodologies and methods? Why? Why not?

Three early career researchers were asked to reflect on the first two questions, and their responses illustrate their positioning and reasons for this:

> I would position myself first and foremost as a social scientist. I am most experienced in the use of qualitative methods but I have some experience of using quantitative methods and I taught the use of SPSS (data analysis program) to students for three years. I am influenced by a range of philosophical approaches to psychology and I align myself with an idealist approach. I believe that there is no absolute truth; only interpretations and degrees of truth from a subjective point of view. For me, the rich detail of participants' responses is the attraction of a qualitative approach, but I do not seek to generalise these responses to other individuals or to develop laws/rules. (Paula)

> I think I see myself as a critical ethnographer – I like to be able to be part of people's lives and try to capture their experience (not a *Carspecken* – an author who has a set way of being a critical theorist) ... critical theorist though. (Jaymera)

> My production as an early childhood education and care teacher led me to be heavily immersed in critical theory. However, as I have obtained more knowledge and experience, I have come to understand the importance of being informed by multiple knowledge-bases and perspectives and also the importance of working within and against what I consider to be true. For me, this is the essence of a *bricoleur* – one who uses different tools, methods, techniques, theories and perspectives to inform understanding. (Kathryn)

Reflection is the key to being able to articulate your research identity, assisting you to clarify underpinning theories you draw from, which provides insight into your own thinking. It helps charts your development as a researcher.

WHAT IMPACT COULD MY RESEARCH HAVE...

...On my own practice and the practice of others?

Research and practice are not mutually exclusive from each other. As Mukherji and Albon (2010) point out, conducting your own research 'is both personally rewarding and important in terms of developing greater understandings of issues relating to young children and their families. Crucially, research is significant in further developing early childhood practice' (p. 249). Generally in the early childhood field, there is a move towards evidence-based practice, which involves the use of research to inform practice, but perhaps even more important is the involvement of practitioners themselves in research. According to Burton and Bartlett (2005), practitioner researchers in the education sector develop 'both their research skills as well as a deeper understanding of the nature of learning, teaching and the educational process' (p. 183). Educators who engage in practitioner research have been reported (Zeichner, 2003) as being more able to critically analyse their teaching, and more confident to make improvements in their work relating to pupil attitudes, involvement, learning and behaviour. Research can become a mechanism for monitoring the efficacy and adequacy of practice decisions and methods. With expectations of increasing accountability, there is an ethical responsibility to monitor the effectiveness of our practice, thereby increasing the competency of, and confidence in, what we do. Being involved in research, one inevitably develops a questioning approach to the work that is undertaken.

For those new to the research process, it can be an enlightening experience where many new skills are developed and findings can be directly applied to practice. For one practising teacher, Mira, who was studying for an honour's degree, the decision to undertake an action research project had direct relevance to her practice. By using action research she was able to focus on an aspect of her own practice that concerned her. Mira studied her verbal interactions with the children she taught during group time from a much more informed perspective. She could see that by working in a certain way she was in fact silencing children who she really wanted to encourage to enter into the group dialogue. The action research cycle allowed her to make subtle changes to her questioning, to implement these changes and then to consider the outcomes, which led to a more favourable response from the children.

For other more experienced researchers, the research process can become quite addictive as each research project generates more questions that need to be answered. This can become very motivating when it directly relates to practice or policy, as research allows the investigation into new areas that perhaps have not been navigated before. A research team comprising early and mid-career researchers in both the health and education fields from Queensland and Victorian universities began researching the area of integrated practice in multi-professional teams in children's services. This was a new concept for Australia and there was little national research available. Through their research, this team was able to build the knowledge-base at a more localised level while also adding to the research literature from overseas studies. This research and the development of accompanying practical resources have since been disseminated to the field and have been applied to practice. These researchers continue their work, but now there is the potential for other related research to increase as more and more interest is generated from the original study, bringing new questions and perspectives.

...On policy development?

Research has the potential to determine 'informed practice', to impact policy and to promote reform. The impact of research on policy development or related initiatives can be direct or indirect. For example, the findings of the longitudinal study conducted in the United Kingdom – *The Effective Provision of Pre-school Education (EPPE) Study* (Sylva, Melhuish, Sammons, Siraj-Blatchford, & Taggart, 2004) – has influenced policy decisions not only in the UK in regards to young children's early education and care experiences, but also in Australia in relation to programming, practice and the early childhood environment. For example, the *Belonging, Being and Becoming: The Early Years Learning Framework for Australia* (DEEWR, 2009) (Australia's first national framework document for the Children's Services sector) draws on this study. Researchers from this significant project have been invited to speak with government officials and have run forums across Australia for educators working in the early childhood education and care field. There remains ongoing government interest in the findings emanating from this study internationally. It would be the wish of many researchers to have their findings acknowledged and taken into consideration when policy is being formed or revised; however, this is not always the case. What is more realistic is to have an influence at a local level and to inform relevant policies in specific workplaces.

A good place to start is influencing policy development in your own organisation by undertaking research that is targeted to the work of your organisation and the issues that it faces. For example, practitioner research can influence decisions about practice and pedagogy. Staff members at an inner-city childcare centre were asked to reflect on their interactions with the children they worked with on a daily basis. The staff hypothesised that there were strong staff–child interactions occurring throughout the day. However, after researching this issue, staff were surprised to see that this was not the case. It became apparent from the findings of the study that for the majority of the time staff were involved in routine tasks such as cleaning, rather than interacting with the children. After reflecting on the findings and trialling a new strategy, which saw one staff member designated as responsible for all routine tasks for a set period of time, allowing other staff in the room to be totally focused on interacting with the children, the centre policy was changed. This example illustrates how practitioners can come together through a collaborative research project to solve a practice issue and influence policy at a localised level.

Impacting policy can occur at a more major level if the research is timely and relevant people and organisations know that the research is occurring. One example of research that has affected the early childhood workforce in one Australian state is the 'Where to from here?: Student Teachers' Career Choices' project. With an aging workforce and increasing staff turnover, there was a need not only to attract, but also to retain, a large number of new teachers. Coupled with this was the commitment of all Australian states and territories to a National Partnership on Early Childhood Education with the Commonwealth Government. This initiative ensured that all children would have access to a quality early childhood education program by the year 2013, delivered by a degree-trained early childhood teacher for 15 hours a week, 40 weeks a year, in the year before formal schooling begins. The workforce situation was critical. In direct response to the government directive and the related workplace issue, researchers at two Victorian universities, Victoria University and the Australian Catholic University, pooled their resources and decided to begin researching the perceived career paths of their pre-service teachers who were undertaking a dual qualification which, on graduation, would enable them to teach in either an early childhood setting or primary school.

Unfortunately, anecdotal evidence suggested that a career in the early childhood sector was not the preferred choice of students undertaking these dual qualification courses, with these graduates being more likely to take up primary teaching positions. With very little evidence existing to inform any future initiatives regarding the promotion of early childhood as a career of choice among the student teacher population, the researchers decided to set up an unfunded research project that focused on exploring the factors influencing the career choices of their pre-service teachers. As the research progressed, the government department in the state of Victoria that was responsible for workforce development became aware of the research and collaborated with the researchers to ensure their findings were considered in the department's response to this issue. Their research was able to inform the development of a pilot program that would challenge the perceptions of pre-service teachers, raising awareness of the unique rewards and opportunities available in early childhood careers and supporting them to develop in their role as an early childhood teacher. Sometimes research beginnings can be about seeing a need and then structuring a research project around that need.

Ideally, you should ensure that you inform others who may benefit from the research findings and keep them aware of your study's progress and eventual findings.

WHERE TO FROM HERE?

Equating the research journey to any other type of journey, it is natural to feel a sense of fulfilment when you think back to what has been achieved, experienced and learnt. However, there may also lurk feelings of sadness that the journey is now over. Like any journey, you may experience mixed feelings once a research project draws to a close. Feelings of sheer relief that you have in fact been able to endure the journey and finish the research project, feelings of adulation and achievement in that you were able to undertake a research project and have findings to share with others, or a sense of mourning in that after being immersed in something so intensively for a period of time it has now come to an end. Take heart, as your journey can continue if you want it to and if you think strategically about it.

In taking your research journey forward, you may sometimes feel as if you are steering into unknown areas. You will need to search for leads in an effort to pin down possible research projects or opportunities you can be involved in. You may consider applying to become a team member on a larger project as a way to begin establishing yourself as a researcher in your field or discipline area. In many cases you will need to be proactive and actively seek out partnerships which hopefully will lead to new research collaborations. What is often required is to spread your net wide and in the right places to connect with further research opportunities. Being proactive means that you might like to consider emailing an esteemed researcher with a similar research interest or research topic to your own. Using email or other social media allows you to take a less direct route than a face-to-face meeting, while still enabling a dialogue to occur. Kym, an early career researcher at the time, contacted a new member of parliament to explain her research findings as the topic related to the minister's portfolio. We, the authors, vividly remember attending our first conferences, where we wanted to approach some of the more well-known researchers but felt unable to due to our perceived low research status. In time, you do summon the courage to approach such people and often are pleasantly surprised by their generosity to talk with you about shared research interests.

Also consider searching for places where your work can be taken up in a practical sense. Think about making your work accessible by using technology such as the internet or social networking (see Chapter 9). One place to begin is to present your research at a conference. Perhaps consider presenting at an international conference sympathetic to your topic or discipline area, where you will have opportunities to discuss your research and the research of others with like-minded people and perhaps plan joint research ventures. Jennifer's story is one example of how presenting at an international conference can be the start of ongoing networking opportunities. It is included here to support you in your decision to present your work in public forums and the possibilities that may spill out from this venture.

Jennifer's thesis related to school-age care and schools. It focused on investigating the circumstances for two school-age care services located on school sites during a time of program expansion, and changes in operation and administration due to mandatory standards and quality assurance measures. At the time of completion, Jennifer was one of the few researchers in her country of residence researching school-age care. She decided to present her work at an international conference as national conferences tended not to embrace the topic because there was little research being conducted in the area. From that one international presentation, Jennifer became connected to international networks, the European Network for School Age Care (ENSAC) as well as the Scottish Out of School Care Network (SOSCN), and she joined an online group comprising international scholars. The presentation also led to an invitation from the Scottish Government to present her thesis findings and an invitation to supervise a doctoral student researching a similar topic in Scandinavia (Iceland). Closer to home, networking continued, with Jennifer making contact with state and national advocacy groups for school-age care programs. Building this profile has also seen Jennifer awarded a tender by the federal government in her home country to develop resources to support reforms in the children's services sector, and she was successful in obtaining a university community partnership grant to begin researching children's perceptions of their time spent in before- and after-school care programs.

While some may look at this profile and say that it is more about being in the right place at the right time, there is no denying that Jennifer has worked tirelessly to promote her research and her passion for the topic, and in doing so has drawn both national and international attention for her work. What we learn from this story is that building your research connections and your profile takes time, persistence and strategic thinking.

Sometimes opportunities happen by chance. For example, you may present the findings of your research at a conference and an audience member approaches you because he/she has similar research interests, and thus a research partnership is formed. At other times you may have to create these opportunities yourself. This is where a mentor can assist, as you have someone to share ideas with about how to advance your research career.

Mentoring is a partnership of support in professional growth (Elliott, 2008). It is an intentional pairing of a more experienced researcher with a novice researcher to achieve a mutually agreed goal or outcome. Mentors traditionally have been seen as assisting in the transmission of knowledge and skills, alongside developing the confidence and competence of their mentees. For this relationship to work there needs to be a level of commitment from both parties. Mentors have to maintain a non-judgemental approach, give time and space, respond to the needs of the mentee, keep confidentiality, believe in the potential of the mentee, and above all be able to recognise the significance of the role and its power (adapted from Elliot, Washburn, Fahey, Mehta, Pond, Ross-Degnan, et al., 2003; Elliott, 2008; Robins, 2009). Mentees have to be realistic in their expectations of the mentor, keep confidentiality and accept responsibilities for the process (Robins, 2009; Zachary, 2005).

Andrea, a mid-career researcher who was fortunate enough to link with an effective mentor early in her research career, saw the need to mentor other researchers. She established a small group which met once a month for two hours in her office. The inaugural members of this group were her higher degree research students. However, membership steadily built as word spread across other universities about the existence of the group. Soon the meeting had to be relocated into a designated meeting room at the university where she worked, due to the increase in member numbers. Membership soon included researchers at the professorial level, mid-career researchers, as well as novice researchers, students studying for higher degrees, and those students undertaking minor research projects as part of their courses. The group voted to be known as the Early Childhood Research Consortium, although the allied health, care and education fields were also represented within the membership. The aim of the group remained true to Andrea's original intention, which was to provide an ongoing space where higher degree students and academics researching in the early childhood field could come together and share their research journeys in a relaxed, supportive environment with the purpose of building research capacity. The meetings were titled 'Talking about early childhood research' and the agenda encouraged contributions from all members no matter what level of research expertise. Numbers grew relatively quickly; from the initial four members, there were 32 members in just two and a half years. Since its establishment, research partnerships have evolved between members of the group as synergies between research interests were uncovered. For example, when Elizabeth, whose research proposal was featured in Chapter 4, joined this group, she found an existing member held a similar interest to her own which enabled the two researchers to design and implement a research project across two universities. Standard agenda items for the monthly meetings included signposting upcoming conferences and, when calls for papers are due, highlighting possible journals to target for the publication of research, the sharing of new publications from members, as well as any current government or policy initiatives that involve early childhood. There is always time for a 'professional conversation' with a guest speaker or a group member presenting their research. Time is set aside specifically for the higher degree students so they can share their experiences – successes or challenges – and this discussion is facilitated by a more experienced researcher or group of researchers.

The way this group functions is indicative of the trend in the literature on mentoring, which indicates a shift from the traditional expert/novice roles, to a more collaborative approach involving co-constructors and learners (Graham, Hudson-Ross, Atkins, McWhorter, & Stewart, 1999). Mentoring used in this way is seen as a more reciprocal undertaking (Black & Puckett, 1996, cited in Pavia, Nissen, Hawkins, Monroe, & Filimon-Demyen, 2003), reflecting the mutuality of learning between mentors and mentees (Clutterbuck, 2004).

AMY AND LARA'S JOURNEYS

To conclude this book we would like to leave the last words to Amy and Lara, who have so generously shared their research journeys with us. Both were asked to discuss what they felt they had gained from the research experience and what opportunities lay ahead from this point onwards. As you read their responses, you will see how they position themselves as researchers, giving us a hint to their perceived professional identity.

Reflecting on her research journey: Amy

After completing my doctorate, I worked for about a year as a contract lecturer in early childhood education at an older 'sandstone' university. While there I was invited to become an 'associate researcher' on a large longitudinal research project. I was then offered an ongoing lecturing position at a newer university, where early childhood education was an expanding area. In this new position, I felt more secure, and that I had more opportunities to develop my academic and research career. I also set about publishing from my thesis. Unfortunately, staffing issues meant that I had to take on extra responsibilities, and some degree of stress, in the areas of teaching and course administration. This meant that for 18 months to two years my writing and research was virtually put on hold. Another difficulty I faced in my research career was that, apart from some wonderful exceptions, initially there was a lack of mentoring and clear opportunities for collaboration with other researchers in my areas of interest. For a while I felt that I was drifting, and that time was running out for me to establish myself as a researcher. I was beginning to panic. Then my university provided some funds for an 'emerging research group', of which I was a member. With these funds, and in collaboration with others, I was able to initiate a couple of small research projects in my areas of interest. All of a sudden I felt that I had found my feet in research, I could call myself a 'Chief Investigator', and I could see pathways and opportunities ahead. Another important support to my research career has been my involvement with an informal 'consortium' of early childhood colleagues across several universities, with similar research interests. This group has enabled the establishment of several research projects, and is a valuable source of fellowship and support.

I have learnt several things about being a teaching academic who is also trying to do research: the importance of finding colleagues to collaborate with, the need for persistence, and the value of starting small. I lost valuable time for a period, but looking back I do not know what I could have done differently in the circumstances. For me, there is frequent conflict between the priorities of meeting students' needs and advancing my research career. But hopefully, as I become more established and practised in research, this conflict will lessen.

While I am still interested in early gifted development, and 'play' will always be a passion for me, I have also found new research interests since I completed my doctorate. I am now interested in doing research that has more immediate practical applications, and that relates to current issues of policy and practice in early childhood education and care, or to my work as an academic. This is in contrast to the more 'theoretical' interest that motivated my doctoral thesis.

Completing the doctoral thesis was a major landmark in my personal and professional life. It really is like a 'rite of passage', and it feels like people look at you differently when you have 'done the thesis'. But it is also just the beginning of a research career that is hopefully driven by the same passion to 'find out' and make a contribution, no matter if it is only small.

Reflecting on her research journey: Lara

Since completing my doctorate in December 2009 I have moved to Australia and pursued an academic career. At first I didn't know where to start looking for post-doc academic roles and to be honest was a little unsure about where I might fit into an existing discipline or research group. I still see myself as a multidisciplinary researcher which has its pros and cons for my research identity. The benefits are being able to see a breadth of practical applications of my work and being able to focus on what interests me the most – the way that people interact with each other. The challenges are finding a research unit or institute to which I fit, and being recognised as a researcher with a future within any one single discipline area.

Finding a post-doc role turned out to be easier than I thought and the university was working with me on that one. I became employed by a small research institute within a university and was soon thrown into the deep end of applying for funding to cover my own salary. This was a huge learning curve and continues to be a challenge. I hadn't learned any of the skills of seeking funding as a doctoral student so was very overwhelmed to begin with. My advice to anyone in the same boat is go for small-seed funding to begin with and concentrate on developing a network and then a smaller cluster of researchers you like working with and from whom ideas flow easily. Concentrate on winning funding designed to develop and refine your ideas and commit to following these smaller projects with larger funding applications. Leave your ego at the door and be prepared to be unnamed on funding applications in the early days, but always ensure you receive due credit within your unit and for any publications you co-author. Pursue your passion and bear in mind that academic research is in many ways a 'back of house' role. Increasingly, though, researchers will need to develop networking and communication skills to make themselves known and have the best chance at obtaining funding.

Research journeys continue as we constantly learn from each new research project, the unique challenges each presents, and the researchers we work with. May your research journey flourish.

REFLECTION POINTS

When reflecting on your own development as a researcher, use the following questions to guide your thoughts:

- What research skills have I gained from undertaking this project?
- Which aspects of the research process did I feel the most confident with?
- Which aspects were the most difficult for me?
- Why do I think this was the case?
- What would I do differently next time?
- What have I learnt about myself as a researcher?
- Who could I collaborate with next time?
- How can I further develop my research skills?

☐ **Summary**

In bringing the research journey to a close, this chapter has focused on the personal and professional growth researchers may experience from being involved in research. Strengths and issues with being part of a research community have been touched on, along with the importance of taking time to reflect on the research journey and what has been learnt. It concludes by considering:

- the impact of research on practice;
- the ability of research to influence policy; and
- where future opportunities for research may lie.

REFERENCES

Althusser, L. (1971). Ideology and the ideological state apparatuses. In L. Althusser, (Ed.), *Lenin and philosophy and other essays* (pp. 127–189). New York: Monthly Review Press.

Anning, A. (2010). 'Research' in early childhood settings: a pause for thought. *Early Years, 30*(2), 189–191.

Arthur, S., & Nazroo, J. (2003). Designing fieldwork strategies and materials. In J. Ritchie & J. Lewis (Eds.), *Qualitative research practice: a guide for social science students and researchers* (pp. 109–137). London: Sage.

Aubrey, C., David, T., Godfrey, R., & Thompson, L. (2000). *Early childhood educational research: issues in methodology and ethics*. London: Routledge Farmer.

Babbie, E. (2010). *The practice of social research*. Belmont, CA: Cengage Learning.

Baumfield, V., Hall, E., & Wall, K. (2008). *Action research in the classroom*. London: Sage.

Bazeley, P. (2003). Computerized data analysis for mixed methods research. In A. Tashakkori & C. Teddlie (Eds.), *Handbook of mixed methods in social science and behavioural research* (pp. 385–422). Thousand Oaks, CA: Sage.

Bell, D. (1973). *The coming of post-industrialised society: a venture in social forecasting*. New York: Basic Books.

Bell, J. (2010). *Doing your research project: a guide for first-time researchers in education, health and social science* (5th edn). Maidenhead, UK: Open University Press.

Best, J., & Kahn, J. V. (2006). *Research in education* (10th edn). Upper Saddle River, NJ: Pearson.

Bolzan, N. P., & Gale, F. (2011). Expect the unexpected. *Child Indicators Research, 4*(2), 269–281.

Brenner, M., Brown, J., & Canter, D. (1985). *The research interview*. London: Academic Press.

Britzman, D. P. (1991). *Practice makes practice: a critical study of learning to teach*. Albany, NY: State University of New York Press.

Bronfenbrenner, U. (1979). *The ecology of human development: Experiments by nature and design*. Cambridge, MA: Harvard University Press.

Brown, P. M. (1997). *Symbolic play and language development in hearing impaired children: the effect of caregiver intervention*. Unpublished doctoral dissertation, University of Melbourne, Victoria, Australia.

Brown, R. (1994). Write right first time. *Literati Newsline*, Special Issue, 1–8. Retrieved October, 2011, from: www.literaticlub.co.uk/writing/articles/write/html.

Bullough, R. V., & Pinnegar, S. (2001). Guidelines for quality in autobiographical forms of self-study research. *Educational Researcher, 30*(3), 13–21.

Bulman, C. (2004). Teachers' and students' perspectives on reflection-on-action. In C. Bulman & S. Schutz (Eds.), *Reflective practice in nursing* (3rd edn) (pp. 128–145). Oxford: Blackwell.

• Burns, R. B. (2000). *Introduction to research methods* (4th edn). South Melbourne, Vic.: Longman.

Burton, D., & Bartlett, S. (2005). *Practitioners research for teachers*. London: Paul Chapman Publishing.

Cann, A., Dimitriou, K., & Hooley, T. (2011). *Social media: a guide for researchers*, from Research Information Network.

Cannella, G. (1997). *Deconstructing early childhood education: social justice and revolution*. New York: Peter Lang.

Caracelli, V. J., & Greene, J. C. (1993). Data analysis strategies for mixed-method evaluation designs, *Educational Evaluation and Policy Analysis, 15*(2), 195–207.

Cartmel, J. (2007). *Outside school hours care and schools*. Unpublished doctoral thesis, Queensland University of Technology, Brisbane, Australia.

Cartmel, J. (2010). *7001HSV research methods* [Podcast]. Griffith University, Gold Coast, Australia.

Clandinin, J. (2006). *Handbook of narrative inquiry: mapping a methodology*. Thousand Oaks, CA: Sage.

Clandinin, D. J., & Connelly, M. (2000). *Narrative inquiry: experience and story in qualitative research*. San Francisco, CA: Jossey-Bass.

Clark, A., & Moss, P. (2001). *Listening to young children: the mosaic approach*. London: National Children's Bureau for the Joseph Rowntree Foundation.

Clough, P., & Nutbrown, C. (2007). *A student's guide to methodology: justifying enquiry*. London: Sage.

Clutterbuck, D. (2004). *Everyone needs a mentor: fostering talent in your organisation* (4th edn). London: Chartered Institute of Personnel and Development.

Cochran-Smith, M., & Donnell, K. (2006). Practitioner inquiry: blurring the boundaries of research and practice. In J. L. Green, G. Camilli, & P. B. Elmore (Eds.), *Handbook of complementary methods in education research* (pp. 503–518). Mahwah, NJ: Lawrence Erlbaum Associates.

Coffey, A. (1999). *The ethnographic self: fieldwork and the representation of identity*. London: Sage.

Cohen, L., Manion, L., & Morrison, K. (2011). *Research methods in education* (7th edn). London: Routledge Falmer.

Corsaro, W., & Molinari, L. (2000). Entering and observing children's worlds: a reflection on a longitudinal ethnography of early education in Italy. In P. Christensen & A. James (Eds.), *Research with children: perspectives and practices* (pp. 179–200). London: Routledge Falmer.

Council of Australian Governments (COAG) (2006). *National Reform Agenda, February, Canberra*. Retrieved November 15, 2011, from: www.alga.asn.au/newsroom/communiques/01.coag/20060210.php.

Creswell, J. (2003). *Research design: qualitative, quantitative and mixed approaches* (2nd edn). Thousand Oaks, CA: Sage.

Crocker, L. (2006). Introduction to measurement theory. In J. L. Green, G. Camilli, & P. B. Elmore (Eds.), *Handbook of complementary methods in education research* (pp. 371–384). Mahwah, NJ: Lawrence Erlbaum Associates.

Crotty, M. (1998). *The foundations of social research: meaning and perspective in the research process.* St Leonards, NSW: Allen & Unwin.

Danby, S. (2002). The communicative competence of young children. *Australian Journal of Early Childhood, 27*, 25–30.

Davis, J. (2009). Involving children. In E. Tisdall, J. Davis, & M. Gallagher (Eds.), *Researching with children and young people: research design, methods and analysis* (pp. 154–167). London: Sage.

DEEWR (Department of Education, Employment and Workplace Relations) (2009). *Belonging, being and becoming: the Early Years Learning Framework for Australia.* Canberra: Commonwealth of Australia.

DEEWR (Department of Education, Employment and Workplace Relations) (2010). *Belonging, being and becoming: educator's guide to the Early Years Learning Framework for Australia.* Canberra: Commonwealth of Australia.

Deitz, J. (1989). Reliability. In L. J. Miller (Ed.), *Developing norm-referenced standardized tests* (pp. 125–148). Binghamton, NY: The Haworth Press.

Denzin, N. K., & Lincoln, Y. S. (2000). The discipline and practice of qualitative research. In N. K. Denzin & Y. S. Lincoln (Eds.), *Handbook of qualitative research* (2nd edn) (pp. 1–45). Thousand Oaks, CA: Sage.

Denzin, N. K., & Lincoln, Y. S. (2011). Introduction: the disciplines and practice of qualitative research. In N. K. Denzin & Y. S. Lincoln (Eds.), *The SAGE handbook of qualitative research* (4th edn) (pp. 1–19). Thousand Oaks, CA: Sage.

Department of Education and Early Childhood Development (DEECD) (2008). *Research priority areas of interest 2008–2011*, Education Policy and Research Division, DEECD, Melbourne, Australia. Retrieved April, 2009 from: www.education.vic.gov. au/about/directions/researchpriority.htm.

DeVellis, R. (1991). *Scale development: theory and applications.* Newbury Park, CA: Sage.

Dewey, J. (1933). *How we think.* Lexington, MA: C. C. Heath. (Original work published 1901.)

Dhillon, P. A. (1999). (Dis)locating thoughts: where do birds go after the last sky. In T. Popkewitz & L. Fendler (Eds.), *Critical theories in education: changing terrains of knowledge and politics* (pp. 191–208). New York: Routledge.

Diaz-Andrade, A. (2009). Interpretive research aiming at theory building: adopting and adapting the case study design. *The Qualitative Report, 14*(1), 42–60.

Dockett, S., & Einarsdottir, J. (2010). Researching with children. *Every Child, 16*(4), 34–35.

Dockett, S., & Perry, B. (2007). *Transitions to school: perceptions, expectations, experiences.* Sydney, NSW: University of New South Wales Press.

Dockett, S., & Perry, B. (2011). Researching with young children: seeking assent. *Child Indicators Research, 4*(2), 231–247.

Dreyfus, H., & Rabinow, P. (1982). *Michel Foucault: beyond structuralism and hermeneutics.* Chicago, IL: The University of Chicago Press.

Dunst, C. J., & Dempsey, I. (2007). Family–professional partnerships and parenting competence, confidence, and enjoyment. *International Journal of Disability, Development and Education*, *54*, 305–318.

Elliott, A. (2006). *Early childhood education: pathways to quality and equity for all children.* Camberwell, Vic.: Australian Council for Educational Research.

Elliott, A. (2008). Mentoring for professional growth. *Every Child*, *14*(3), 7.

Elliot, K., Washburn, S., Fahey, P., Mehta, S., Pond, C., Ross-Degnan, L. et al. (2003). *Supporting early childhood professionals through content-focused mentoring: a resource guide.* Centre for Children and Families, Education Department Centre. Retrieved July, 2008, from: https://secure.edc.org/publications/prodview.asp?1583.

Emerson, R. (2001). *Contemporary field research* (2nd edn). Long Grove, IL: Waveland Press.

Emerson, R., Fretz, R., & Shaw, L. (1995). *Writing ethnographic fieldnotes.* Chicago, IL: The University of Chicago Press.

Fielding, M., & Bragg, S. (2003). *Students as researchers: making a difference.* Cambridge: Pearson.

Foucault, M. (1978). Governmentality. Place: Publisher. Reprinted in G. Burchell, C. Gordon, & P. Miller (Eds.) (1991), *The Foucault effect* (pp. 87–104). London: Harvester Wheatsheaf.

Foucault, M. (1979). *Discipline and punish.* London: Penguin.

Foucault, M. (1980). Truth and power. In C. Gordon (Ed.), *Power/knowledge: selected interviews and other writings, 1972–77, by Michel Foucault* (pp. 109–133). New York: Pantheon Books.

Foucault, M. (1983). On the genealogy of ethics: an overview of work in progress. In H. Dreyfus & P. Rabinow (Eds.), *Michel Foucault: beyond structuralism and hermeneutics* (pp. 229–252). Chicago, IL: The University of Chicago Press.

Foucault, M. (1984a). Nietzsche, genealogy and history. In P. Rabinow (Ed.), *The Foucault reader* (pp. 76–100). London: Penguin.

Foucault, M. (1984b). Technologies of the self. In P. Rabinow (Ed.), *Michel Foucault, ethics: essential works of Foucault 1954–1984* (Vol. 1) (pp. 223–251). London: Penguin.

Foucault, M. (1985). The use of pleasure: the history of sexuality (Vol. 2). New York: Pantheon Books.

Foucault, M. (1991). The politics and the study of discourse. In G. Burchell, C. Gordon, & P. Miller (Eds.) (1991), *The Foucault effect* (pp. 53–72). London: Harvester Wheatsheaf.

Fraser, N. (1989). *Unruly practices: power, discourse and gender in contemporary social theory.* Cambridge: Polity Press.

Gadamer, H. G. (2006). Language and understanding. *Theory, Culture and Society*, *23*(13), 13–27.

Gallagher, M. (2009). Data collection and analysis. In E. Tisdall, J. Davis, & M. Gallagher (Eds.), *Researching with children and young people: research design, methods and analysis* (pp. 65–88). London: Sage.

Gans, H. (1999). Participant observation in the era of 'ethnography'. *Journal of Contemporary Ethnography*, *28*(5), 540–548.

Geetz, C. (1973). *The interpretation of cultures: selected essays.* New York: Basic Books.

● Genzuk, M. (2003). *A synthesis of ethnographic research.* Retrieved September 23, 2003, from: www-rcf.usc.edu/~genzuk/Ethnographic_Research.html.

Gerson, K., & Horowitz, R. (2002). Observation and interviewing: options and choices in qualitative research. In T. May (Ed.), *Qualitative research in action* (pp. 199–224). London: Sage.

Gibbons, M., Limoges, C., Nowotny, H., Schwartzman, S., Scott, P., & Trow, M. (1994). *The new production of knowledge: the dynamics of science and research in contemporary societies.* London: Sage.

Gil, F., & Jover, G. (2000). Las tendencias narrativas en pedagogía y la aproximación biográfica al mundo infantile. *Enrahonar, 31,* 107–122.

Gordon, C. (Ed.). (1980). *Power/knowledge, selected interviews and other writings, 1972–1977, by Michel Foucault.* New York: Pantheon Books.

Gottfried, A. W., Eskeles Gottfried, A., Bathurst, K., & Wright Guerin, G. (1994). *Gifted IQ early developmental aspects: The Fullerton Longitudinal Study.* New York: Plenum Press.

Graham, P., Hudson-Ross, S., Atkins, C., McWhorter, P., & Stewart, J. (1999). *Teacher/mentor: a dialogue for collaborative learning.* New York: Teachers College Press.

Greene, J. (2007). *Mixed methods in social inquiry.* San Francisco, CA: Jossey-Bass.

Greene, S., & Hill, M. (2005). Researching children's experience: methods and methodological issues. In S. Greene & D. Hogan (Eds.), *Researching children's experience: approaches and methods* (pp. 1–21). London: Sage.

Greig, A., Taylor, J., & MacKay, T. (2007). *Doing research with children* (2nd edn). London: Sage.

Grieshaber, S., & Cannella, G. (2001). *Embracing identities in early childhood.* New York: Teachers College Press.

Guba, E. G. (1981). Criteria for assessing the trustworthiness of naturalistic inquiries. *Educational Communication and Technology, 29*(2), 75–91.

Guba, E. G., & Lincoln, Y. S. (1994). Competing paradigms in qualitative research. In N. K. Denzin & Y. S. Lincoln (Eds.), *Handbook of qualitative research* (pp. 105–117). London: Sage.

Hand, H. (2003). The mentor's tale: a reflexive account of semi-structured interviews. *Nurse Researcher, 10*(3), 15–27.

Harrington, B. (2003). The social psychology of access in ethnographic research. *Journal of Contemporary Ethnography, 32*(5), 592–625.

Harris, A. (2011). *Ethnocinema in arts education: intercultural collaboration in film.* Doctoral dissertation title: *Cross-marked: Sudanese Australian young women talk education* (book and films). The Netherlands: Springer SBM. Retrieved September, 2011 from: www.springer.com/series/7472?detailsPage=titles.

Hart, C. (2005). *Doing a literature review.* London: Sage.

Hatch, J. A. (2007). *Early childhood qualitative research.* New York: Routledge.

Hatcher, C. (1997). *Making the enterprising manager in Australia: a genealogy.* Doctoral dissertation, Queensland University of Technology, Brisbane, Australia.

Herrington, J., & Oliver, R. (1999). Using situated learning and multimedia to investigate higher-order thinking. *Journal of Educational Multimedia and Hypermedia, 8*(4), 401–421.

Holstein, J., & Gubrium, J. (2003). *Inside interviewing: new lenses, new concerns.* London: Sage.

Hsiu-Zu, H., O'Farrell, S., Hong, S., & You, S. (2006). Developmental research: theory, method, design and statistical analysis. In J. L. Green, G. Camilli, & P. B. Elmore (Eds.), *Handbook of complementary methods in education research* (pp. 207–225). Mahwah, NJ: Lawrence Erlbaum Associates.

Jackson, A. (2009). *Listening to children's experience of starting year one in an area of socio-economic disadvantage.* Unpublished manuscript, School of Human Services and Social Work, Griffith University, Logan, Queensland, Australia.

Jenks, C. (1996). The postmodern child. In J. Brannen & M. O'Brien (Eds.), *Children in families: research and policy* (pp. 13–25). London: Falmer Press.

Johnny, L. (2006). Reconceptualizing childhood: children's rights and youth participation in schools. *International Education Journal, 7*(1), 17–25.

Johnson, B. H. (2000). Family-centred care: four decades of progress. *The Journal of Collaborative Family Health Care, 18*(2), 137–156.

Jones, S., Torres, V., & Arminio, J. (2006). *Negotiating the complexities of qualitative research in higher education: fundamental elements and issues.* New York: Routledge.

Jover, G., & Thoilliez, B. (2011). Biographical research in childhood studies: exploring children's voices from a pedagogical perspective. *Child Indicators Research, 4*(2), 119–129.

Kamler, B. (2010, December 14). *Developing authority in writing-for-publication.* PD session help at Victoria University, Melbourne, Australia.

Kamler, B., & Thomson, P. (2006). *Helping doctoral students write: pedagogies for supervision.* Abingdon, Oxon: Routledge Falmer.

Kant, I. (1966). *Critique of pure reason.* Garden City, NY: Doubleday. (Original work published 1781.)

Keen, D. (2007). Parents, families, and partnerships: issues and considerations. *International Journal of Disability, Development and Education, 54,* 339–349.

Kellett, M. (2010). *Rethinking children and research: attitudes in contemporary society.* New York: Continuum.

Kervin, L., Vialle, W., Herrington, J., & Okely, T. (2006). *Research for educators.* South Melbourne, Vic.: Cengage Learning.

Kinchloe, J., & McLaren, P. (2000). Rethinking critical theory and qualitative research. In N. K. Denzin & Y. S. Lincoln (Eds.), *Handbook of qualitative research* (2nd edn) (pp. 279–314). Thousand Oaks, CA: Sage.

Kinney, L. (2006). Small voices powerful messages many interpretations. Retrieved March 1, 2010 from: www.ltscotland.org.uk/Images/listeningtochildren_tcm4-234433.pdf.

Krippendorff, K. (1980). *Content analysis.* London: Sage.

Kruger, T., Davies, A., Eckersley, B., Newell, F., & Cherednichenko, B. (2009). *Effective and sustainable university–school partnerships.* Canberra: Teaching Australia.

Langston, A., Abbott, L., Lewis, V., & Kellett, M. (2004). Early childhood. In S. Frawer, V. Lewis, S. Ding, M. Kellett, & C. Robinson (Eds.), *Doing research with children and young people* (pp. 147–160). London: Sage.

Lather, P. (1996, April). *Methodology as subversive repetition: practices toward a feminist double science.* Paper presented at the American Educational Research Association Conference, New York.

Laws, S., with Harper, C., & Marcus, R. (2003). *Research for development*. London: Sage.

Lawson, H. (1985). *Reflexivity*. La Salle, IL: Open Court.

Legard, R., Keegan, J., & Ward, K. (2003). In-depth interviews. In J. Ritchie & J. Lewis (Eds.), *Qualitative research practice: a guide for social science students and researchers* (pp. 138–169). London: Sage.

Lévi-Strauss, C. (1966). *The savage mind* (2nd edn). Chicago, IL: The University of Chicago Press.

Lincoln, Y. S., & Guba, E. G. (1985). *Naturalistic inquiry*. Beverly Hills, CA: Sage.

Lofland, J., & Lofland, L. (1995). *Analyzing social settings: a guide to qualitative observation and analysis*. Belmont, CA: Wadsworth.

Lowe, B., Winzar, H., & Ward, S. (2007). *Essentials of SPSS: a business approach*. Melbourne, Vic.: Thomson.

Lundy, L. (2007). 'Voice' is not enough: conceptualizing Article 12 of the United Nations Convention on the rights of the child. *British Educational Research Journal, 33*(6), 927–942.

Lyotard, J. F. (1984). *The postmodern condition*. Manchester: Manchester University Press.

Macfarlane, K. (2006). An analysis of parental engagement in contemporary Queensland schooling. Doctoral dissertation, Queensland University of Technology, Brisbane, Australia.

Macfarlane, K., & Cartmel, J. (2008). Playgrounds of learning: valuing competence and agency in birth to three-year-olds. *Australian Journal of Early Childhood, 33*(2), 41–47.

Macfarlane, K., Cartmel, J., & Nolan, A. (2011). Developing and sustaining pedagogical leadership. Retrieved September, 2011, from: www.ecceleadership.org.au.

Mackey, G., & Vaealiki, S. (2011). Thinking of children: democratic approaches with young children in research. *Australasian Journal of Early Childhood, 36*(2), 83–86.

MacLure, M., & Walker, B. (2007). Interrogating the discourse of home–school relations: the case of 'parents' evenings. In M. Hammersley (Ed.), *Educational research and evidence-based practice* (pp. 220–244). London: Sage.

MacNaughton, G., & Hughes, P. (2009). *Doing action research in early childhood studies: a step-by-step guide*. Maidenhead, UK: Open University Press.

MacNaughton, G., Rolfe, S., & Siraj-Blatchford, I. (2010). *Doing early childhood research: international perspectives on theory and practice* (2nd edn). Crows Nest, NSW: Allen & Unwin.

Malaguzzi, L. (1993). History, ideas and basic philosophy. In C. Edwards, L. Gandini and G. Forman, *The hundred languages of children: The Reggio Emilia approach to early childhood education*. Norwood, NJ: Ablex. ED 355 034.

Mason, J. (2002a). *Qualitative researching*. London: Sage.

Mason, J. (2002b). Qualitative interviewing: asking, listening and interpreting. In T. May (Ed.), *Qualitative research in action* (pp. 225–241). London: Sage.

Mason, J., & Dale, A. (2011). *Understanding social research: thinking creatively about method*. London: Sage.

Maxwell, J. A. (1996). *Qualitative research design: an interactive approach*. Thousand Oaks, CA: Sage.

Mayall, B. (2002). *Towards a sociology for childhood: thinking from children's lives*. Buckingham, UK: Open University Press.

Maynard, M. (1994). Methods, practice and epistemology: the debate about feminism and research. In M. Matnar & J. Purvis (Eds.), *Researching women's lives* (pp. 10–26). London: Taylor & Francis.

McCain, M., & Mustard, F. (1999). *Early years study – final report*. Toronto: Ontario Children's Secretariat.

McLeod, J. (2000, June). *Qualitative research as bricolage*. Paper presented at the Society for Psychotherapy Research Annual Conference, Chicago, IL.

McQueen, R., & Knussen, C. (2006). *Introduction to research methods and statistics in psychology*. Sydney, NSW: Prentice Hall.

Meadmore, D., Hatcher, C., & McWilliam, E. (2000). Getting tense about genealogy. *The International Journal of Qualitative Studies in Education, 13*(5), 463–479.

Meredyth, D., & Tyler, D. (1993). *Child and citizen: genealogies of schooling and subjectivity*. Brisbane, Queensland: Institute for Cultural and Policy Studies, Griffith University.

Merriam, S. (1998). Analytic techniques and data management. In S. Merriam (Ed.), *Qualitative research and case study applications in education* (pp. 155–170). San Francisco, CA: Jossey-Bass.

Merriam, S. (2002). *Qualitative research in practice*. San Francisco, CA: Jossey- Bass.

Miles, M. B., & Huberman, A. M. (1994). *Qualitative data analysis* (2nd edn). Thousand Oaks, CA: Sage.

Miller, W., & Crabtree, B. (2004). Depth interviewing. In S. Hesse-Biber & P. Leavy (Eds.), *Approaches to qualitative research: a reader on theory and practice* (pp. 185–202). Oxford: Oxford University Press.

Mishler, E. (1990). Validation in inquiry-guided research: the role of exemplars in narrative studies. *Harvard Educational Review, 60*, 415–442.

Mukherji, P., & Albon, D. (2010). *Research methods in early childhood: an introductory guide*. London: Sage.

Murray, R. (2009). *Writing for academic journals*. Maidenhead, UK: Open University Press.

Narayan, U. (1988). Working together across difference: some considerations on emotions and political practice. *Hypatia, 3*(2), 31–48.

Neuman, W. L. (2007). *Basics of social research: qualitative and quantitative approaches*. Boston, MA: Pearson.

Newman, L., & Pollnitz, L. (2002). *Professional, ethical and legal issues in early childhood*. Frenchs Forest, NSW: Pearson.

Nolan, A., & Sim, J. (2011). Exploring and evaluating levels of reflection in pre-service early childhood teachers. *Australasian Journal of Early Childhood, 36*(3), 122–130.

O'Hara, M., Carter, C., Dewis, P., Kay, J., & Wainwright, J. (2011). *Successful dissertations: the complete guide for education, childhood and early childhood studies students*. London: Continuum.

Olesen, V. L. (2000). Feminisms and qualitative research at and into the millennium. In N. K. Denzin & Y. S. Lincoln (Eds.), *Handbook of qualitative research* (2nd edn) (pp. 215–256). Thousand Oaks, CA: Sage.

Pallant, J. (2011). *SPSS survival manual* (4th edn). Crows Nest, NSW: Allen & Unwin.

Pavia, L., Nissen, H., Hawkins, C., Monroe, M. E., & Filimon-Demyen, D. (2003). Mentoring early childhood professionals. *Journal of Research in Childhood Education, 17*(2), 250–260.

Piaget, J. (1951). *Play, dreams and initiation in childhood*. New York: Norton.

Ponterotto, J. G. (2005). Qualitative research in counselling psychology: a primer on research paradigms and philosophy of science. *Journal of Counselling Psychology, 52*(2), 126–136.

Prout, A. (2005). *The future of childhood*. Abingdon, Oxon: Routledge Falmer.

Punch, K. F. (2009). *Introduction to research methods in education*. London: Sage.

Raghavendra, P., Murchland, S., Bentley, M., Wake-Dyster, W., & Lyons, T. (2007). Parents' and service providers' perceptions of family-centred practice in a community-based, paediatric disability service in Australia. *Child: Care, Health & Development, 33*(5), 586–592.

Rasmusson, B. (2011). Children's advocacy centres (Barnahus) in Sweden: experiences of children and parents. *Child Indicators Research, 4*(2), 301–321.

Riches, G., & Dawson, P. (2002). Shoestrings and *bricolage*: some notes on researching the impact of a child's death on family relationships, *Death Studies, 26*, 209–222.

Ritchie, J., & Lewis, J. (2003). *Qualitative research practice: a guide for social science students and researchers*. London: Sage.

Robins, A. (2009). *Mentoring in the early years*. London: Sage.

Rogoff, B. (2003). *The cultural nature of human development*. New York: Oxford University Press.

Ropers-Huilman, B. (1999). Witnessing: critical inquiry in a poststructural world. *Qualitative Studies in Education, 12*(1), 21–35.

Rose, N. (1990). *Governing the soul: the shaping of the private self*. London: Routledge.

Rose, N. (1999). *Powers of freedom: reframing political thought*. Cambridge: Cambridge University Press.

Rose, N. (2000). Community, citizenship and the third way. *American Behavioural Scientist, 43*(9), 1395–1411.

Rourke, L., Anderson, T., Garrison, R., & Archer, W. (2001). Methodological issues in the content analysis of computer conference transcripts. Retrieved November 17, 2005, from: http://aied.inf.ed.ac.uk/members01/archive/vol_12/rourke/full.html.

Sacks, H. (1984). On doing 'being ordinary'. In J. Atkinson & J. Heritage (Eds.), *Structures of social action: studies in conversation analysis* (pp. 413–429). Cambridge: Cambridge University Press.

Scheeres, H., & Solomon, N. (2000). Research partnerships at work: new identities for new times. In J. Garrick & C. Rhodea (Eds.), *Research and knowledge at work* (pp. 178–199). London: Routledge.

Schonkoff, J. P., & Phillips, D. A. (2000). *From neurons to neighbourhoods: the science of early childhood development*. Washington, DC: National Academy Press.

Schwandt, T. A. (2000). Three epistemological stances for qualitative inquiry: interpretivism, hermeneutics, and social constructionism. In N. K. Denzin & Y. S. Lincoln (Eds.), *Handbook of qualitative research* (2nd edn) (pp. 189–213). Thousand Oaks, CA: Sage.

Siemon, D. (2002). Developing an early childhood policy framework. Paper presented at the Children's Welfare Association of Victoria, Melbourne, Australia.

Silverman, D. (2003). *Interpreting qualitative data: methods for analysing talk, text and interaction*. London: Sage.

Smith, J. A. (2007). Hermeneutics, human sciences and health: linking theory and practice. *International Journal of Qualitative Studies on Health and Wellbeing*, 2, 3–11.

Stagnitti, K. (2003). The development of an assessment of pretend play. Unpublished doctoral thesis, Deakin University, Melbourne, Victoria.

Stewart, R. (2001, September). Practice v. praxis: Constructing models for practitioner-based research. Paper presented at the ACUADS Conference, Adelaide, Australia.

Swadener, B. B. (2005). Kenyan street children speak through their art. In L. D. Soto & B. B. Swadener (Eds.), *Power and voice in research with children* (pp. 137–149). New York: Peter Lang.

Sylva, K., Melhuish, E., Sammons, P., Siraj-Blatchford, I., & Taggart, B. (2004). *The Effective Provision of Pre-School Education (EPPE) project: final report*. London: Department for Education and Skills/Institute of Education.

Taber, K. S. (2007). *Classroom-based research and evidence-based practice: a guide for teachers*. London: Sage.

Tamboukou, M., & Ball, S. J. (2003). *Dangerous encounters: genealogy and ethnography*. New York: Peter Lang.

Taylor, M. C. (2005). Interviewing. In I. Holloway (Ed.), *Qualitative research in health care* (pp. 37–55). Maidenhead, UK: Open University Press.

Thoilliez, B. (2011). How to grow up happy: an exploratory study on the meaning of happiness from children's voices, *Child Indicators Research*, 4(2), 323–351.

Thomas, J. (1993). Doing critical ethnography. *Qualitative Research Methods Series*, No. 26. Newbury Park, CA: Sage.

Tisdall, E. K. M., Davis, J. M., & Gallagher, M. (2009). *Researching with children and young people: research design, methods and analysis*. London: Sage.

Tong, R. (1989). *Feminist thought: a comprehensive introduction*. London: Routledge.

Touraine, A. (1984). The waning sociological image of social life, *International Journal of Comparative Sociology*, 25(1–2), 33–44.

Tyler, D. (1993). Making better children. In D. Meredyth & D. Tyler (Eds.), *Child and citizen: genealogies of schooling and subjectivity* (pp. 35–60). Brisbane, Queensland: Institute for Cultural and Policy Studies, Griffith University.

Tyler, D., & Johnson, L. (1991). Helpful histories, *History of Education Review*, 20(2), 1–8.

United Nations (1989). *United Nations Convention on the Rights of the Child*. Geneva: United Nations.

Van Maanen, J. (1988). *Tales of the field: on writing ethnography*. Chicago, IL: The University of Chicago Press.

Veale, A. (2005). Creative methodologies in participatory research with children. In S. Greene & D. Hogan (Eds.), *Researching children's experience: approaches and methods*. London: Sage.

Viruru, R., & Cannella, G. S. (2001). Postcolonial ethnography, young children and voice. In S. Grieshaber & G. Cannella (Eds.), *Embracing identities in early childhood*. New York: Teachers College Press.

Vygotsky, L. S. (1978). *Mind in society: the development of higher psychological processes*. Cambridge, MA: Harvard University Press.

Walford, G. (2001). *Doing qualitative educational research: a personal guide to the research process*. London: Continuum.

Wellington, J. (2003). *Getting published: a guide for lecturers and researchers*. London: Routledge Falmer.

Wheedon, C. (1997). *Feminist practice and poststructuralist theory* (2nd edn). Oxford: Blackwell.

Wolcott, H. F. (1994). *Transforming qualitative data: description, analysis, and interpretation*. Thousand Oaks, CA: Sage.

Woodhead, M. (2006). Changing perspectives on early childhood: theory, research and policy. Paper commissioned for the EFA Global Monitoring Report 2007, Strong Foundations: Early Childhood Care and Education. Retrieved August, 2011 from: http://unesdoc.unesco.org/images/0014/001474/147499e.pdf.

Yates, L. (2005). *What does good education research look like?* Maidenhead, UK: Open University Press.

Zachary, L. J. (2005). *The mentors guide: facilitating effective learning relationships*. San Francisco, CA: Jossey-Bass.

Zeichner, K. M. (2003). The adequacies and inadequacies of three current strategies to recruit, prepare, and retain the best teachers for all children, *Teachers College Record*, *105*, 490–519.

INDEX